Reporting for SAP Asset Accounting

Thomas Michael

MW00978364

Contents

Contents

Preface

SAP's Asset Accounting module, which is a subsidiary ledger to the General Ledger and is used for the management and accounting of fixed assets, is used by over 15,000 companies worldwide. All of these companies use it to track, manage, depreciate, and otherwise account for their fixed assets. The fundamental purpose of the module is to produce various reports for fixed assets to support general ledger account balances, management decisions, tax filings, and physical property tracking.

As an SAP consultant since 1994, I have helped over 60 companies worldwide implement the Asset Accounting module. During this time, I have seen my clients struggle with different functionalities of the Asset Accounting system, including intelligent global designs, worldwide rollouts, or simple user procedures. All of my clients, however, struggle with one common issue: reliable and meaningful reporting.

My clients typically complain that Asset Accounting reporting is everything from cumbersome to slow, and from inaccurate to inaccessible. Once I inquire about the details, however, I almost invariably find that it is not really the Asset Accounting report that is causing the problem, but rather a lack of practical instructions. Useful documentation is sparse at best and most users have never received any formal Asset Accounting reporting training – even the standard SAP training class only scratches the surface of the reporting features. It is therefore my hope that this guide will fill the reporting knowledge gap.

There are so many Asset Accounting reports and reporting queries in the SAP system that it would be impossible to cover them all in just one guide. Many of these reports only apply to certain countries or statutory requirements; others are older, out-of-date reports; and yet others are internal SAP correction and analysis reports. Fortunately, you probably only need a handful of reports to provide accurate, reliable, and accessible asset information. This guide will cover these most common Asset Accounting reports and their features and functionalities.

Assumptions

While researching and writing this guide, I have made some assumptions about you, the reader. I am guessing that you work with Asset Accounting on a more or less daily basis, be it as an asset accountant or asset manager doing day-to-day asset management work, a super user who's involved in supporting the Asset Accounting module, a representative from the tax department pulling together supporting evidence for IRS filings, or a consultant, whose job it is to design, configure, and implement the Asset Management system. Whichever the case may be, your interest is likely in learning about the basic reporting capabilities for Asset Accounting.

Furthermore, I suspect that you already have basic SAP knowledge that covers general navigation procedures and standard features such as selection screen criteria, etc. In addition, you probably have basic accounting knowledge and understand the terms used in the Asset Management business.

> **Note**
>
> Please note that this guide is based on *SAP Enterprise Resource Planning (SAP ERP)* Release 6.0. Most reports and reporting features, however, are available in previous releases as well.

How This Guide Is Organized

This guide consists of eight chapters, each of which is divided into several sections. I will cover reporting basics first and then explore the details of several specific Asset Accounting reports. Let's now review the chapters of this guide so that you can get an idea of what you will learn in each chapter. Knowing how the guide is organized can help you decide how you would best like to use the guide, for example, whether to proceed chapter-by-chapter, or in a more modular fashion.

Preface
In this preface, I explain the need for this reporting guide and provide you with an orientation for the remaining chapters. An overview of each chapter is also included.

Chapter 1: Basic Asset Accounting Reporting Features
Chapter 1 explains the basics of asset reporting, including report selection screens, and how to work with dynamic selections, sort versions, and Microsoft Excel® downloads. Understanding the basic reporting features unique to Asset Accounting reports will be instrumental in your understanding the material in the remainder of this guide.

Chapter 2: Asset Balance Reports
In Chapter 2, we will explore the details for the most important balance-based asset reports for Asset Accounting, including the Asset Balance report, the Asset Portfolio report, the Total Depreciation report, the Posted Depreciation report and the Depreciation Forecast report. Each report description includes detailed information about the report's features, main purpose and function, as well as menu path and transaction code.

Chapter 3: Asset Transaction Reports
Chapter 3 explains the most important transaction-based reports for Asset Accounting, including the Asset Acquisition report, the Asset Retirement report, the Asset Transfer report, the Asset Transaction report, and the List of Origins by Asset Debits report. Detailed descriptions include menu path, transaction code, and main purpose and function for each report.

Chapter 4: Asset History Sheet Report
In Chapter 4, you will learn about the required configuration and detailed reporting and layout features for the Asset History Sheet report, the most important and powerful report available for fixed assets. You will learn why this report is so important and how to configure it to meet your specific reporting requirements.

Chapter 5: Asset Specialty Reports
Chapter 5 will introduce you to certain specialty reports, which are delivered in the standard asset reporting system, such as the Barcode report, the Physical Inventory List report, the Asset Master Data Changes report, the Asset History report, the Real Estate and Similar Rights report, the Transportation Equipment report, the Leasing report, and the Insurance Values report. These reports are not like the typical asset value reports explained in Chapters 2 and 3. Instead, these reports provide information about physical pieces of equipment, specialty assets, and the changes that have been made to them.

Chapter 6: US Tax Reports
In Chapter 6, you'll explore the standard reports specifically delivered for US Tax reporting purposes, including the Mid-Quarter Alert report, the Depreciation Comparison report, and the Net Worth Valuation report. You'll learn how these reports can help you to compile the necessary asset information and values when the time for tax filing comes around.

Chapter 7: Reporting Tools
Chapter 7 will introduce you to additional reporting tools available for Asset Accounting, including Simulation Versions and Currency Translation Methods. These tools help you go beyond the basic reporting options for fixed assets. You will learn how you can use them to provide advanced reports in any currency and how to answer what-if scenarios.

Chapter 8: Asset Explorer
Chapter 8 introduces you to the Asset Explorer. This tool lets you perform comprehensive reporting and analysis for a single asset, including depreciation forecasting, currency translations, and transaction simulation.

Resources
The Resources list provides you with links to additional asset reporting information on the Internet. There is a wealth of information available online and I have compiled a list of the most useful links for you to learn more about Asset Accounting reporting.

Outside of the Scope of This Book

In addition to the standard fixed asset reports provided within the SAP system, many clients use a Business Information Warehouse (BW) application for asset reporting as well. BW is a great reporting application, but it goes beyond the scope of this book. For in-depth BW coverage, I suggest that you take a look at the SAP PRESS book *SAP BW Reporting and Analysis*.

Where to Go from Here

Reporting for Asset Accounting is an important topic. Without it, year-end close activities, tax returns, asset tracking, and management decisions would be negatively impacted.

In Chapter 1, we will explore the basic reporting features unique to Asset Accounting reports. It is important to understand these features as they serve as a foundation for producing accurate asset reports.

Acknowledgements

Writing this guide has truly been a team effort and thus, I'd like to thank the following people: John Jordan for convincing me to write this guide; my editors Jawahara Saidullah and Jutta VanStean for making the book-writing process as easy as possible on me; my friend Kent Bettisworth for his continued professional advice; and most importantly, the entire Asset Accounting development team at SAP in Walldorf (I'm not naming any names – you know who you are!) for all your help, advice and friendship over the last 12 years – without you I wouldn't be where I am now. And finally, my wife Michelle for putting up with the long hours and week-ends!

1 Basic Asset Accounting Reporting Features

As an introductory step to learning about the most commonly used asset accounting reports in the chapters that follow, Chapter 1 will explain in detail some of the basic reporting features for fixed assets. Understanding and utilizing these features is the basis for comprehending and efficiently using any reporting solution.

1.1 Logical Database ADA

Before we get into the details of Asset Accounting reporting, let's talk about a feature in SAP products called *Logical Databases*. A *Logical Database* (LogDB) is a group of complex ABAP programs designed to perform efficient data retrieval from various database tables. Put simply, the LogDB reads all asset information, including master data, values, and transactions, and it does so in a very efficient manner.

Having worked as a consultant for a number of years, I have met many people, mostly from technical teams, that consider Logical Databases to be the root of all evil. Nothing, however, could be further from the truth since the Logical Database plays a critical part in asset reports. In fact, most, if not all, standard Asset Accounting reports use the Logical Database ADA (which is the asset-specific LogDB) for data selection, amount calculations, and reporting output.

Most modules in SAP products have their own LogDB; for example, the Logical Database for the Investment Management module is IMA, and for the Project System module it's PSJ.

The Importance of the LogDB in Asset Accounting
When using the Asset Accounting reports, LogDB is the tool of choice for all standard asset reports. Why? Because you use it for asset information selection and, more important, it calculates all asset values (i.e., net book value at the beginning of the fiscal year, total annual depreciation amount, etc.) for you automatically.

Other Uses of the LogDB
You might be surprised to learn that the most commonly used asset values, such as the acquisition cost or the net book value, aren't stored in the asset database tables, but are calculated at runtime. The LogDB is responsible for all of these calculations.

Should you ever consider creating a custom ABAP report or an ABAP query, you must ensure that you use the LogDB as the basis for all selections and amount calculations. In this way, you can ensure that the amounts calculated in your custom report match the corresponding amounts in the standard reports, because you're using the same formulas stored in the LogDB.

Accessing the LogDB ADA
If you want to learn more about the LogDB for fixed assets, do the following:
1 Go to Transaction **SE36** and enter "ADA".
2 Click **Display** to see the structure of the LogDB.

Figure 1.1 shows you what tables are included in the LogDB and their relationship to each other.

> **Note**
> You can find more information about LogDB on SAP's help website at **http://help.sap.com • mySAP ERP • SAP ERP Central Component • English** or by following this link:
> *http://help.sap.com/saphelp_erp2005vp/helpdata/en/4f/71e1d0448011d189f00000e81ddfac/frameset.htm.*

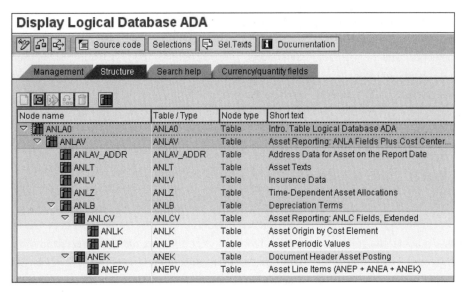

Figure 1.1 LogDB ADA Structure

1.2 The Basic Selection Screen

As was mentioned in Section 1.1, the LogDB is used in almost all asset reports. In addition to master data selection and amount calculations, the LogDB also provides the basic selection criteria screens for all reports.

The selection screens used for the various standard Fixed Asset reports are very similar; many of them are actually identical. In fact, the LogDB ADA for Asset Accounting includes just a handful of variations of the basic selection screen.

Every report starts with a basic selection screen that allows users to limit their reports to certain selection criteria, such as assets, asset classes, date ranges, etc. In this section, we'll take a close look at the basic selection screen and its features.

> **Note**
> In Chapters 2 and 3, we'll go over the details for each asset report and identify any specific selection screen features that are different from the basic screen.

Short (Abbreviated) and Full Version of the Basic Selection Screen

It is important to know that each selection screen has two versions:

▶ A full version

▶ A short (abbreviated) version

Figure 1.2 shows the basic selection screen in its short version. This abbreviated version includes a limited range of selection fields. For example, in this case, only the **Asset class** field is available as a selection criterion in the **Selections** section.

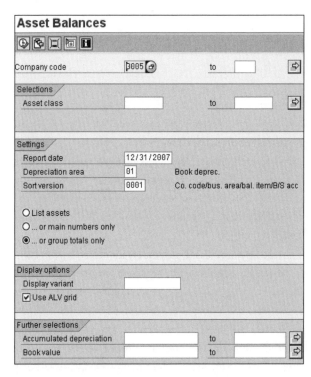

Figure 1.2 Basic Selection Screen – Short Version

You can switch easily from a short selection screen to its full version by clicking the button labeled **All Selections**.

Figure 1.3 shows the basic selection screen for most Asset Accounting reports in its full version, which includes all basic selection fields. You will notice that the **Selections** section now includes several additional fields such as the **Business area**, **Cost center**, **Plant**, etc.

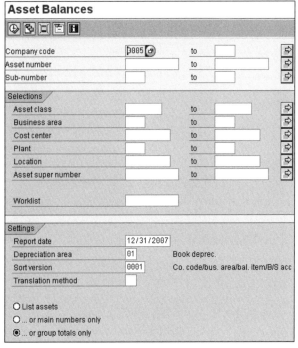

Figure 1.3 Basic Selection Screen – Full Version

Basic Selection Screen Elements

The basic selection screen has several elements, including unique identifiers and the **Selections** and **Settings** sections. Let's look at these elements in more detail.

Unique Identifiers

Because any fixed asset is uniquely identified by the combination of **Company code**, **Asset number**, and **Sub-number**, almost every report includes these three fields at the very beginning of a selection screen. This makes it easy to limit a report to just certain assets. For example, many companies use different number ranges for certain assets (i.e., Asset under Construction (AuC) could begin with an asset number of '9,' while buildings might start with a '2,' etc.).

Selections

Next, the basic selection screen includes a section labeled **Selections**, which contains the most commonly used fields of an asset master record, such as **Asset class**, **Cost center**, **Plant**, etc. All of these fields refer to the information stored in the asset master record (as opposed to the asset's values). The buttons to the right of the selection fields allow for multiple selections, such as complex inclusions and exclusions by range or individual values.

Settings

The **Settings** section includes very important report parameters such as the **Report date**, **Depreciation area**, and **Sort version**. Furthermore, it contains the **Translation method** parameter. Let's look at each parameter in more detail.

▶ **Report date**

The **Report date** parameter determines that the asset values are to be calculated and displayed as of that date. Depending on the report you use, you can't enter just any date here. You have to consider three different scenarios for entering this date, which we'll now look at in detail.

Note

For the purpose of simplification, I am using a fiscal year equal to the calendar year (01/01–12/31) in all of the examples in this guide.

▶ **Report date in the current fiscal year**

You can enter any date that falls on the last day of a period. For example, assuming a standard calendar year, you could enter 1/31, 2/28, and 3/31, for example, as report dates, because they all fall on the last day of a period (or month). If you were to enter a mid-month date such as 3/15 or 4/10, the system would issue an error message (Message AU117 – Report Date invalid). These are not valid report dates because they don't fall on the last day of a period. Similarly, entering the first day of a period (3/1 or 7/1, etc.) would result in the same error message being issued.

There is one exception to this rule. When you enter the first day of the fiscal year as the report date, the system uses the last day of the prior fiscal year to run the report. In other words, if you entered 1/1/2008 as a report date, the system would use 12/31/2007 instead. This ensures that the values reported at the beginning of a year would equal the values at the end of the previous fiscal year.

▶ **Report date for prior fiscal years**
In this scenario, you have to differentiate between two separate cases:

▶ *Prior fiscal years are already closed in Asset Accounting*
If the fiscal year you're trying to run the report for is already closed, the system allows only the last day of the fiscal year as the report date. Again, assuming a standard calendar year, you would only be able to use 12/31 as the reporting date. All other dates (end of a month, and middle or beginning of a month) would result in an error message (Message AU116 – Report Date invalid for closed fiscal years). The reason why Asset Accounting won't let you run reports for prior closed fiscal years, with a report date other than the last day of the fiscal year, is that it would cause the Logical Database to recalculate asset values for the time period specified (i.e., if you enter 9/30 as the report date, the LogDB would recalculate the asset values from 1/1 – 9/30). Now, if the depreciation terms for an asset have changed since that timeframe, the system would calculate new asset values in the report, which wouldn't match the original amounts calculated in the prior fiscal year.
Conversely, when you use the last day of the fiscal year as the report date, the LogDB doesn't have to recalculate any values since the end-of-the-year amounts have already been stored in the database tables (i.e., table ANLC – Asset Summary Value table).

▶ *Prior fiscal years are still open in Asset Accounting*
If the prior fiscal years are still open in the Accounting modules, you can enter any end-of-the-period date as the reporting date (e.g., 3/31 or 6/30, etc.). Using any other report date will result in an error message (Message AU117 – Report Date invalid).

▶ **Report date in future fiscal years**
The rules for running reports for future fiscal years are similar to those for closed fiscal years. The system allows you to enter only the last day of the fiscal year as the report date. If you're using a standard calendar year, you can enter any future fiscal year for your report. However, if you're using any other fiscal year versions (i.e., a 4-4-5 or year-dependent fiscal year), you can only use the future fiscal years that have been maintained in your fiscal calendar. For example, if your fiscal calendar is maintained all the way through 2009, you can run asset reports up to that year. If you tried to run a report for any of the following years, the system wouldn't be able to calculate asset values and therefore would issue an error message.

▶ **Depreciation area**
The **Depreciation area** field in the **Settings** section is another very important report parameter. An asset can have up to 99 different depreciation areas and each depreciation area is for tracking a different set of asset values. For example, depreciation area 01 could be used to track the asset values according to US GAAP (Generally Accepted Accounting Principles) valuation and accounting principles, while depreciation area 10 could be used to track the same asset's US federal tax values. Depreciation area 30 could be used to track the asset's consolidated group values based on another statutory accounting principle (i.e., if asset consolidation is done according to German GAAP accounting rules).
It is therefore critical that you choose the correct depreciation area when running a report. You must always ask yourself: Who is the intended recipient of this report? For example, if you're running a report for your tax department, you should be using a tax-specific depreciation area such as depreciation area 01. If you're running a report to use for reconciliation purposes between the General Ledger and the Asset Accounting subledger, you should be using depreciation area. If, on the other hand, your report is for supporting consolidation values, you should use depreciation areas 30 or 31 (assuming the standard Chart of Depreciation setup).

▶ **Sort version**

Another important parameter in the **Settings** section is the **Sort version** since it controls the sort and subtotals of the report output. In fact, the **Sort version** parameter is so important for the overall quality of any asset report that it warrants going over the details of using sort versions and how to set them up in configuration later on in this chapter in Section 1.5.

▶ **Translation method**

The **Translation method** can be used to display the asset values in any currency required (if left blank, the report will show the asset values in the default currency as specified in the configuration for the **Depreciation area**). Setting up various currency translation methods is a powerful way to run asset reports in any currency using a wide variety of exchange rates. You will learn more about currency translations in Chapter 7.

▶ **Other Options**

Lastly, the **Settings** section lets you specify the detail level of the report, using the following options:

▶ **List assets**

Select this option to specify that you want to see individual asset numbers. If you want to run the report for a limited number of assets only, you should select this option. Note that this list includes asset main numbers and subnumbers.

▶ **…or main numbers only**

This option works just like the **List assets** option, however, it only shows the main number (subnumbers are totaled up and rolled into the main number).

▶ **…or group totals only**

This option allows you to see group totals as defined by the sort version you have selected. If you have a significant number of asset records, you should select this option.

Note

The term *group totals* refers to the sort and subtotal settings in the sort version used. For example, let's say that you entered a sort version that sorts and subtotals by company code and asset class (i.e., in the standard SAP system, this is sort version 0007). When you run the report with the **…or group totals only**

---

option, you would get one subtotal for each asset class and one overall total for each company code that you included in the report. If you run the same report with a different sort version (i.e., sort version 0014 – sort and sub-total by cost center), you would get one sub-total line for each cost center included in the report. The two reports would add up to the same overall total amount, but would look completely different due to the different sort versions.

Now, we'll look at the second part of the basic selection screen (see Figure 1.4).

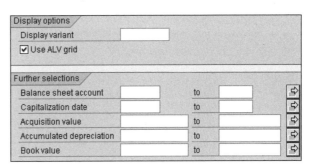

Figure 1.4 Basic Selection Screen – Display Options

Display Options

The **Display options** section allows you to turn the Advanced List Viewer (ALV) display option on or off and use a specific **Display variant** you may have already created. We'll look at the ALV display option in more detail later in this chapter.

Further Selections

Next, the basic selection screen includes the **Further selections** section, which contains the following other commonly used selection fields:

▶ **Balance sheet account** (the asset cost account)

▶ **Capitalization date**

▶ **Acquisition value**

▶ **Accumulated depreciation**

▶ **Book value**

The value fields in this section refer to the asset values as opposed to the fields in the **Selections** section, which refer to the information stored in the asset master record. You should also note that all these values would be calculated as of the reporting date you enter.

1.3   Dynamic Selections

In addition to the fields displayed on the basic selection screen (as explained in the previous section), all standard Asset Accounting reports offer what are called *Dynamic selections*. Dynamic selections provide additional fields for selection on the reporting screen.

These fields include additional asset master record fields and certain administrative information (e.g., the name of the user who created the asset master record, the date/time of creation, who last changed the asset record, etc.). You can call the dynamic selections by clicking the corresponding icon as shown in Figure 1.5.

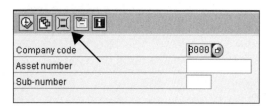

Figure 1.5   Dynamic Selections Icon

Once you invoke the dynamic selections, a secondary window displays on top of the selection screen, which offers a list of additional selection fields. These fields include almost all fields of the asset master record, however, a few important fields are not available. I will explain the reason for this shortly.

Dynamic selections are organized according to the screen layout of the standard asset master record. For example, the asset master record contains a **Net Worth Tax** tab for the list of fields available on this tab (see Figure 1.6).

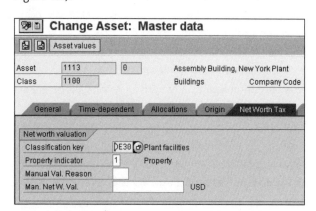

Figure 1.6   Net Worth Tax Screen for the Asset Master Record

Tracking Property Tax Information

The **Net Worth Tax** tab is used to track certain property tax information for asset master records (Net Worth Tax is an awkward translation for Property Tax). Generally speaking, the fields on this tab are not available on the basic selection screen of asset reports.

These fields are, however, available as dynamic selections in asset reports, as shown in Figure 1.7 in the section **Net worth valuation**.

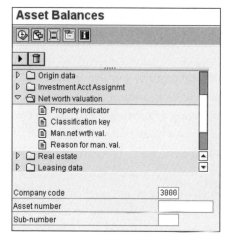

Figure 1.7   Dynamic Selections – Net Worth Valuation

Using Dynamic Selections

To use any of the fields listed under the **Dynamic selections** shown in Figure 1.8, perform the following steps:

1 Select the field.
2 Click the **Copy** icon (this is the icon with the right-facing black triangle/arrow, to the left of the icon with the trash can symbol).

The field will then appear as an additional selection criterion. For example, select the field **Property indicator** as shown in Figure 1.8 and click the **Copy** icon. Asset Accounting will show the **Property indicator** in a separate box to the right as a dynamic selection criterion.

In addition to the most commonly used fields that are included in the asset master record, the dynamic selections also have a section called **Administrative Data,** as shown in Figure 1.9. This section includes helpful fields such as the name of the user who created the asset, as well as the creation date.

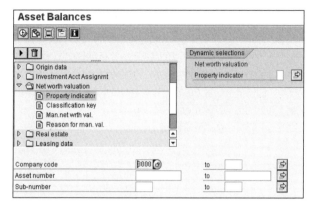

Figure 1.8 Dynamic Selections – Property Indicator

Also available are the **Changed by** and **Changed on** fields, as well as deletion and lock indicators. These fields can be useful when analyzing who has changed an asset or when an asset was changed. See Figure 1.9 for the list of **Administrative Data** fields.

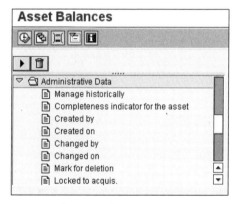

Figure 1.9 Dynamic Selections – Administrative Data

The Useful Life Field

Remember that I said earlier almost all fields are available as dynamic selections? Well, one field that is suspiciously missing from the list of available dynamic selections is the Useful life field. Unfortunately, SAP did not include it in the dynamic selections and, consequently, none of the standard SAP Fixed Asset reports allow you to use the Useful life as a selection criterion.

Since Useful life is quite an important field in asset reporting, specifically for tax reporting purposes, I suggest that you create a custom query or ABAP report that includes the Useful life field in the selection screen.

Other Fields That Are Not Included

Other fields that are not included in the dynamic selections are the Depreciation Key (this field is available on the basic selection screen of the Total Depreciation report, however – see Chapter 3), Depreciation Start Date (not available on any report), and various other depreciation fields. Again, a custom query or ABAP report would be a possible workaround for this (or the use of BW).

1.4 The Advanced List Viewer (ALV)

As of SAP ERP 6.0, most standard Asset Accounting reports are Advanced List Viewer (ALV)-enabled. ALV provides a user interface, which enables dynamic output of reports. Without ALV, the standard Asset Accounting report outputs are static lists, meaning that after the report has been run, users can no longer modify the output. Figure 1.10 shows an example of the **Asset Balances** report without the ALV function.

Notice that the display columns are fixed (i.e., you cannot add, delete, or modify the existing columns), no additional sort or subtotals are possible, and you can't add any fields to the report. Moreover, advanced download functions (such as Excel or Word downloads) are also not available.

Compare that report output to the ALV-enabled report shown in Figure 1.11. It's the exact same report, albeit the ALV option is turned on. Notice that you can resize all columns, as well as add or delete columns if you want. You can also sort and subtotal this report using any column.

Furthermore, you can download this report directly into other office applications (such as Microsoft Excel or Microsoft Word), email this report, or create a graphic chart and add fields to it by using the icons in the application bar. The ALV makes all these functions possible.

To run an ALV-enabled report, ensure that you have selected the option **Use ALV grid** on the basic selection screen of the report as shown in Figure 1.12.

Creating Custom Report Layouts

Another great feature of ALV reports is that they let users create a custom report layout. For example, the first two columns of the report show the asset main number and

Asset Balances

| | | | Assets | Break down grp.asset | | Create worklist | Add to worklist |

Report date: 12/31/2007 Asset Balances - 01 Book deprec. Creation date: 03/05/2007

CompanyCode 3000

Main number	SNo.	Cap. date	Name	Acq.value	Accum.dep.	Book val
1105	0	11/01/1993	Distribution center Seattle	850,369.00	254,112.00-	596,257.00
1106	0	01/01/1993	Administration Building, Los Angeles	31,888,830.00	9,528,878.00-	22,359,952.00
1107	0	12/05/1994	Sales Office South	773,250.00	202,334.00-	570,916.00
1109	0	01/01/1995	Extension Loading Ramp South	126,000.00	32,760.00-	93,240.00
1111	0	12/31/1996	Administration Building II, Los Angeles	86,687.92	19,146.92-	67,541.00
1112	0	01/01/1993	Production Building 1, New York Plant	996.56	229.56-	767.00
1113	0	01/01/1993	Assembly Building, New York Plant	3,188,883.00	952,892.00-	2,235,991.00
1114	0	03/01/1993	Production Building, Chicago Plant	2,125,922.00	635,266.00-	1,490,656.00
1115	0	10/01/1993	Production Building, Atlanta Plant	2,551,106.00	762,322.00-	1,788,784.00
1116	0	01/01/1993	Production Building, Los Angeles Plant	1,062,961.00	497,640.00-	565,321.00
1117	0	01/01/1994	Plant I - Warehouse Central Street	484,570.00	135,688.00-	348,882.00
1118	0	01/01/1993	Plant site, Los Angeles	15,667,260.00	0.00	15,667,260.00
1119	0	10/01/1993	Plant site, Atlanta	7,833,630.00	0.00	7,833,630.00
1120	0	11/09/1994	Real Estate Jefferson Avenue	3,577,000.00	0.00	3,577,000.00
CompanyCode	3000		IDES US INC *	70,217,465.48	13,021,268.48-	57,196,197.00

Figure 1.10 An Asset Balances Report without the ALV Display Option

Asset Balances

Asset	SNo.	Capitalized on	Asset description	Acquis.val.	Accum.dep.	Book val.	Crcy
1105	0	11/01/1993	Distribution center Seattle	850,369.00	254,112.00-	596,257.00	USD
1106	0	01/01/1993	Administration Building, Los Angeles	31,888,830.00	9,528,878.00-	22,359,952.00	USD
1107	0	12/05/1994	Sales Office South	773,250.00	202,334.00-	570,916.00	USD
1109	0	01/01/1995	Extension Loading Ramp South	126,000.00	32,760.00-	93,240.00	USD
1111	0	12/31/1996	Administration Building II, Los Angeles	86,687.92	19,146.92-	67,541.00	USD
1112	0	01/01/1993	Production Building 1, New York Plant	996.56	229.56-	767.00	USD
1113	0	01/01/1993	Assembly Building, New York Plant	3,188,883.00	952,892.00-	2,235,991.00	USD
1114	0	03/01/1993	Production Building, Chicago Plant	2,125,922.00	635,266.00-	1,490,656.00	USD
1115	0	10/01/1993	Production Building, Atlanta Plant	2,551,106.00	762,322.00-	1,788,784.00	USD
1116	0	01/01/1993	Production Building, Los Angeles Plant	1,062,961.00	497,640.00-	565,321.00	USD
1117	0	01/01/1994	Plant I - Warehouse Central Street	484,570.00	135,688.00-	348,882.00	USD
1118	0	01/01/1993	Plant site, Los Angeles	15,667,260.00	0.00	15,667,260.00	USD
1119	0	10/01/1993	Plant site, Atlanta	7,833,630.00	0.00	7,833,630.00	USD
1120	0	11/09/1994	Real Estate Jefferson Avenue	3,577,000.00	0.00	3,577,000.00	USD
Company Code 3000				70,217,465.48	13,021,268.48-	57,196,197.00	USD

Figure 1.11 An Asset Balances Report with the ALV Display Option

subnumber. Let's say you want to add a column in the first position to show the Company code. To do this, click the Change Layout button (this button looks like a spreadsheet icon), then select **Company code** from the list of fields and click the **Copy** button. To save this custom layout, click the **Save layout** button (this button looks like a spreadsheet with a floppy disk icon). You could then select this **Display variant** in the **Display options** section shown in Figure 1.12.

Figure 1.12 The ALV Display Option on the Basic Selection Screen of a Report

ALV and Hierarchical Reports

ALV does have one downside, however. It doesn't work for hierarchical reports (such as the Asset Transaction report, the Asset Acquisitions report, and the Asset

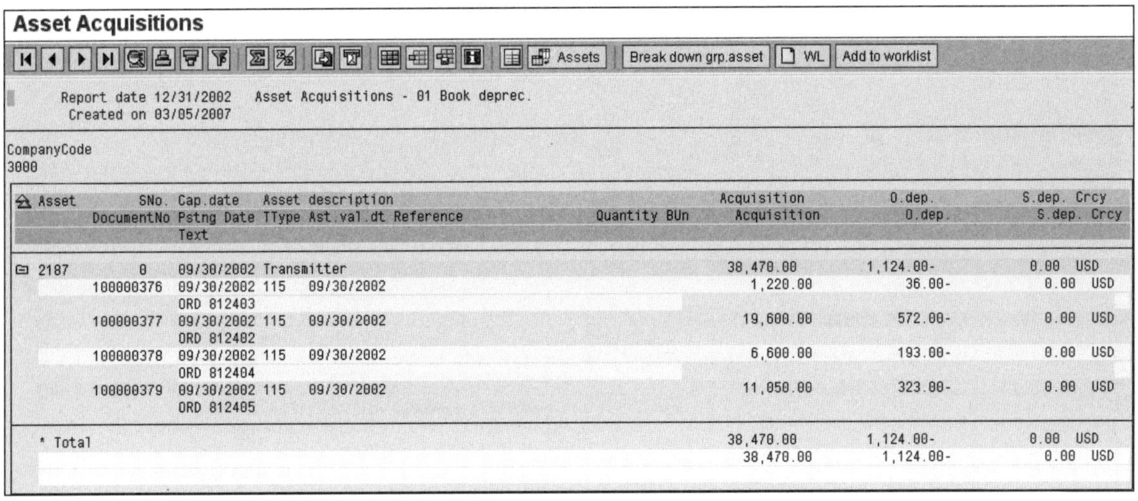
Asset Acquisitions
Assets
Break down grp.asset
WL
Add to worklist
Report date 12/31/2002 Asset Acquisitions - 01 Book deprec.
Created on 03/05/2007
CompanyCode
3000
Asset SNo. Cap.date Asset description Acquisition O.dep. S.dep. Crcy
DocumentNo Pstng Date TType Ast.val.dt Reference Quantity BUn Acquisition O.dep. S.dep. Crcy
Text
2187 0 09/30/2002 Transmitter 38,470.00 1,124.00- 0.00 USD
100000376 09/30/2002 115 09/30/2002 1,220.00 36.00- 0.00 USD
ORD 812403
100000377 09/30/2002 115 09/30/2002 19,600.00 572.00- 0.00 USD
ORD 812402
100000378 09/30/2002 115 09/30/2002 6,600.00 193.00- 0.00 USD
ORD 812404
100000379 09/30/2002 115 09/30/2002 11,050.00 323.00- 0.00 USD
ORD 812405
* Total 38,470.00 1,124.00- 0.00 USD
38,470.00 1,124.00- 0.00 USD

Figure 1.13 Asset Acquisitions Report – Example of a Hierarchical Report

Retirement or Asset Transfer reports). Hierarchical reports show an asset master record and beneath it a number of transactions.

A good example is the **Asset Acquisitions** report shown in Figure 1.13. Notice that the asset **2187** shows four **Acquisition** postings. This report is considered to be hierarchical because the posting transactions are on a lower level than the master record. Unfortunately, ALV doesn't support such reports and the system will automatically switch to the classic layout.

1.5 Sort Versions

Almost every Asset Accounting report allows you to specify a sort version on the basic selection screen. As was already mentioned, *sort versions are very important.* In fact, they are critical to your report output, because they determine what your report will look like and what fields or columns you can add to your report after you have executed it. They also determine whether the report will display asset subnumbers or just an asset main number total, and what sort level will show up with a subtotal. Yet, many users simply accept the default sort version and never get to unlock the power of the standard Asset Accounting reports.

Sort Version Configuration Screen

To understand how sort versions work, let's look at the configuration screen for a sort version. Figure 1.14 shows the configuration screen of the standard Asset Accounting **Sort version 0007**, which sorts and subtotals asset reports by company code and asset class.

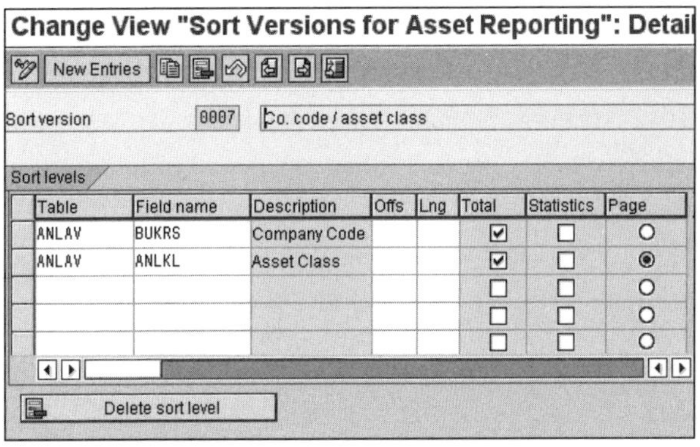
Change View "Sort Versions for Asset Reporting": Detail
New Entries
Sort version 0007 Co. code / asset class
Sort levels
Table Field name Description Offs Lng Total Statistics Page
ANLAV BUKRS Company Code
ANLAV ANLKL Asset Class
Delete sort level

Figure 1.14 The Configuration Screen for Sort Version

To access the configuration for sort versions, go to Transaction **OAVI**, or use the menu path **IMG • Financial Accounting • Asset Accounting • Information System • Define Sort Versions for Asset Reports**.

As you can see, this sort version uses the two fields **Company Code** and **Asset Class** as sort levels. They are specified with their technical names (**Company Code** = **ANLAV-BUKRS** and **Asset Class** = **ANLAV-ANLKL**).

Furthermore, sort levels control the order of the report output. In this case, all assets will be sorted by company code, and then by asset class. Additionally, the sort version will produce a total line for each sort level as indicated by the selected **Total** checkbox. This particular sort version will output a sub-total for each asset class and another overall total for the company code.

Displaying Additional Fields

The fact that this sort version uses the two fields **Company Code** and **Asset Class** will make these two fields available in any asset report as additional fields that can be displayed as a column.

For example, the basic **Asset Balances** report does not include a column that shows the asset class for each asset – see Figure 1.15.

Asset Balances

Asset	SNo.	Cap.date	Asset description	Σ	Acquis.val.
1105	0	11/01/1993	Distribution center Seattle		850,369.00
1106	0	01/01/1993	Administration Building, Los Angeles		31,888,830.00
1107	0	12/05/1994	Sales Office South		773,250.00
1109	0	01/01/1995	Extension Loading Ramp South		126,000.00
Company Code 3000				▪	**33,638,449.00**

Figure 1.15 Asset Balances Report

But because this report uses standard sort version 0007, which includes the asset class field, we can now add this field to the report. To do so, perform the following steps:

1. Click the **Change Layout** (CTRL + F8) icon. This opens the **Change layout** dialog box shown in Figure 1.16, which lists on the right side under **Column Set** all of the available fields you can add to the report (in this case the **Asset Class** field).

> **Note**
> Remember, the list of fields in the **Column Set** section is controlled by the sort version you use. If, for example, sort version 0014 (sort by cost center) had been

used, the **Column Set** section would show the cost center as a field available to add to the report.

2. Select the appropriate field in the **Column Set** section and click the left arrow icon. This adds the field to the **Displayed Columns** section of the window.
3. Click the **Transfer** icon (green checkmark) to finalize the change.

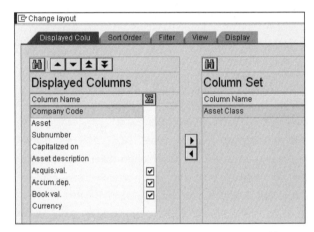

Figure 1.16 Changing the Layout to Add the Asset Class Field to a Report

The result, shown in Figure 1.17, is the same report as before, but with the asset class information available in an additional column, named **Class**.

As you can see, choosing the correct sort version is critical to producing meaningful reports in Asset Accounting.

Therefore, make sure that your sort version includes the fields that you want to display, in addition to the standard fields on any asset report. In other words, the sort version controls which additional fields you can display in an asset report.

Asset Balances

CoCd	Class	Asset	SNo.	Cap.date	Asset description	Σ	Acquis.val.	Σ	Accum.dep.	Σ	Book val.
3000	1100	1105	0	11/01/1993	Distribution center Seattle		850,369.00		254,112.00-		596,257.00
		1106	0	01/01/1993	Administration Building, Los Angeles		31,888,830.00		9,528,878.00-		22,359,952.00
		1107	0	12/05/1994	Sales Office South		773,250.00		202,334.00-		570,916.00
		1109	0	01/01/1995	Extension Loading Ramp South		126,000.00		32,760.00-		93,240.00
	1100					▪	33,638,449.00	▪	10,018,084.00-	▪	23,620,365.00
3000						▪▪	33,638,449.00	▪▪	10,018,084.00-	▪▪	23,620,365.00

Figure 1.17 Asset Balances Report with the Class Column Displayed

Limitations

There are, of course, certain limitations inherent to this functionality. You can only include fields in the sort version that are available in the sort version configuration Transaction **OAVI**.

> **Note**
>
> If you want to include additional fields that are not available in Transaction **OAVI**, you have to do a little coding. You can read OSS note 335065 for more information.

1.6 Microsoft Excel Download

Most standard ALV-enabled reports include a direct download link to Microsoft's Excel® application. This allows you to manipulate asset data easily for further reporting, or to upload asset information into another software application (e.g., tax software, property tax interfaces, consolidation systems, etc.).

In fact, most asset reports not only interface with Microsoft Excel, but also with other standard office appli-

cations such as Microsoft Word®, Microsoft Access® and email applications.

Figure 1.18 shows the standard **Asset Balances** report using sort version 0013 (sorted and sub-totaled by company code) and with the **List asset** option selected. Simply click the icon labeled **Spreadsheet** to download this report to Excel automatically.

When you click the icon, Excel starts in a new window. Asset Accounting will then automatically download all asset data into the Excel spreadsheet – see Figure 1.19.

> **Note**
>
> Notice that Asset Accounting did not download any subtotals or overall totals (i.e., the grand total by company code is shown on the report in the Asset Accounting system, but is not included in the Microsoft Excel spreadsheet). Also, Asset Accounting will not download any filter criteria or custom sorting to Microsoft Excel. This makes it easier to work with the data in Microsoft Excel since the spreadsheet contains only asset data.

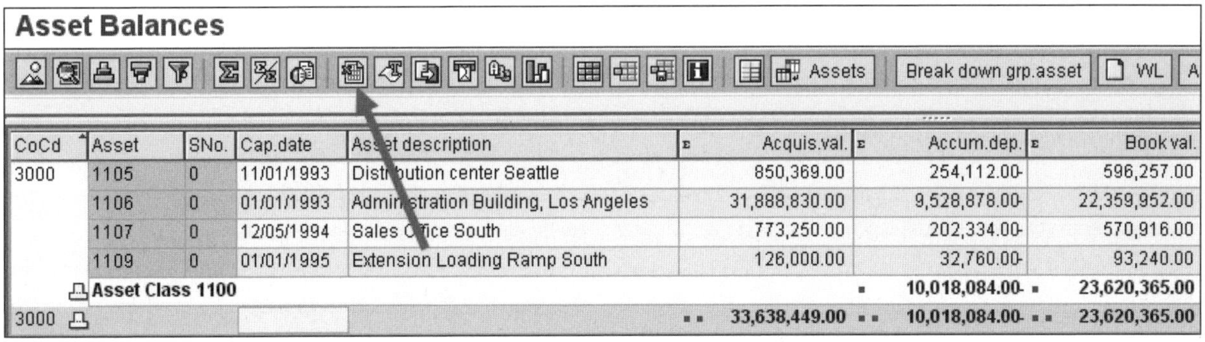

Figure 1.18 Asset Balances Report – Excel Download Icon

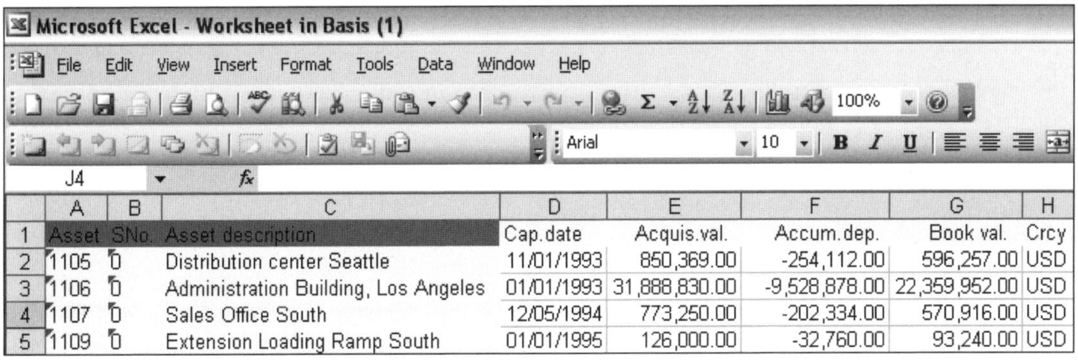

Figure 1.19 Asset Balances Report Downloaded Directly to Excel

	C	D	E	F	G	H	I	J
1	Asset description	Cap.date	APC FY start	Dep. FY start	Bk.val.FY strt	Acquisition	Retirement	Transfer
2	Distribution center Seattle	11/01/1993	850,369.00	-237,104.00	613,265.00	0.00	0.00	0.00

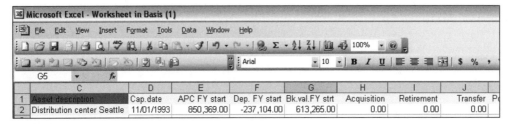

Figure 1.21 Single-Row Download into Microsoft Excel

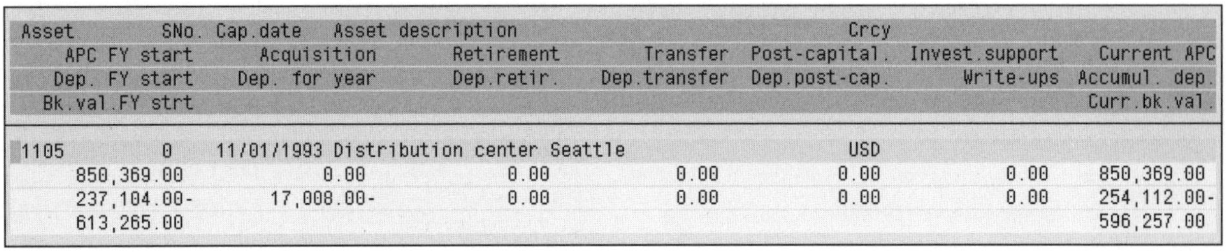

Asset SNo. Cap.date	Asset description			Crcy		
APC FY start	Acquisition	Retirement	Transfer	Post-capital.	Invest.support	Current APC
Dep. FY start	Dep. for year	Dep.retir.	Dep.transfer	Dep.post-cap.	Write-ups	Accumul. dep.
Bk.val.FY strt						Curr.bk.val.
1105 0 11/01/1993	Distribution center Seattle			USD		
850,369.00	0.00	0.00	0.00	0.00	0.00	850,369.00
237,104.00-	17,008.00-	0.00	0.00	0.00	0.00	254,112.00-
613,265.00						596,257.00

Figure 1.20 Old Multi-line Layout for the Asset History Sheet Report

Multi-Line to Single-Line Conversion

Another helpful feature of the new Microsoft Excel download functionality in ERP Release 6.0 is the fact that the download will now convert multi-line reports in Asset Accounting to single-line reports in Microsoft Excel. For example, Figure 1.20 shows the old Asset History Sheet report (also referred to as the Asset Roll-Forward report since it shows the beginning balances at the start of the year, all asset activity for the year, and the ending balances of the end of the year).

As you can see, the report displays the information for asset 1105 in four lines. In earlier Asset Accounting releases, the Microsoft Excel download function would have transferred the data in four rows to Excel, which renders it almost useless for further manipulation or data analysis.

In ERP Release 6.0, the system now uses a single-row format for this report and also downloads the data to Microsoft Excel in a single-row format, which makes further data manipulation and reporting a breeze. See Figure 1.21, where all values for asset **1105** are now shown in a single row.

1.7 Chapter Summary

In this chapter, which lays down the foundation for the remainder of the book, you learned about the most important reporting features of the Asset Accounting module. Hopefully, you now have a better understanding of Asset Accounting. The important points to remember from this chapter are:

- The LogDB ADA is used in almost all standard Asset Accounting reports and is responsible for all data selections and value calculations.
- Additionally, the LogDB controls the basic selection screen for each report.
- Most asset reports use the same or a very similar basic selection screen.
- The Report Date, Depreciation Area, and Sort Version are the most important settings for any report.
- Dynamic Selections are available in all standard Asset Accounting reports and provide additional fields for selection.
- The Advanced List Viewer (ALV) enables dynamic report outputs that can be changed by users, even after a report has been run.
- ALV provides a direct download functionality to Microsoft Excel and other Microsoft Office applications.
- Sort versions not only provide the sort and subtotal levels for a report, but also control the list of available fields that can be added to a report.

In Chapter 2, you'll learn about the most commonly used balance-based asset reports.

2 Asset Balance Reports

The standard reports in SAP Asset Accounting can be grouped into three main categories:

▶ **Balance-based reports**
These reports show the asset balances (such as acquisition cost, accumulated depreciation, net book value, etc.) as of a specific date (the reporting date).

▶ **Transaction-based reports**
These reports show posted transactions for assets for a specific time period (as opposed to a specific point in time as with balance-based reports). The time period usually is year-to-date, but can also be mid-year (i.e., second quarter, July – December, etc).

▶ **Other reports**
These reports include hybrid reports like the Asset History Sheet report (which is both balance- and transaction-based) or master data reports (such as the Asset Change report).

In this chapter, we'll discuss the most important balance-based reports for fixed assets. For each report, you'll find the menu path to execute the report and the transaction code used to start it. In addition, you'll find the technical report name listed.

> **Note**
> If you're anything like me, you probably dread going through a long menu path to find the right report. Over the years, I have managed to memorize the technical report names (and they haven't changed since the early days in Asset Accounting), and now use the following shortcut from anywhere in the SAP system to start any report:
> **System • Service • Reporting**
> From there you can enter the technical report name in the **Program** field, as shown in Figure 2.1, and click the

Execute icon (green checkmark icon, without text). Lastly, I also execute asset reports directly via Transaction **SE38**. If you don't have the proper authorization to run Transaction **SE38**, alternatively, you can use Transaction **SA38**.

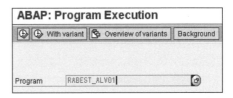

Figure 2.1 Execute Asset Reports Directly via Transaction SA38

Each report description also includes the main purpose of or recipient for the report and a detailed explanation of the reports' features and functions.

2.1 Asset Balances Report

The first report we'll look at is the *Asset Balances* report. This report is probably the most widely used report in Asset Accounting, because of its simple and easy to understand layout. The report shows the acquisition cost, accumulated depreciation, and resulting net book value for an asset as of the reporting date. In addition, the report includes the asset main number and subnumber, capitalization date, and description by default.

The information required to access the Asset Balances report is as follows:

▶ **Menu Path**
Accounting • Financial Accounting • Fixed Assets • Information System • Reports on Asset Accounting • Asset Balances • Balance Lists • Asset Balances

▶ Transaction Code
S_ALR_87011963
▶ Technical Report Name
RABEST_ALV01

2.2 Asset Portfolio (Current Book Value)

As you will see, the *Asset Portfolio* report is seemingly identical to the Asset Balances report (i.e., it has the same technical name); however, it has a different transaction code and menu path. I'll explain this in more detail in a moment. The report itself works just like the Asset Balances report and the output for both reports is also identical.

The information required to access the Asset Portfolio report is as follows:

Main Report Purpose and Recipients

The Asset Balances report provides a simple asset listing that includes the company code, asset main number and subnumber, capitalization date, and description. The report also includes the acquisition cost, life-to-date depreciation, and net book value. The main recipients of this report are general Asset Accounting departments.

Report Output

See Figure 2.2 for the default Asset Balances report output. It is important to notice that all values in this report are as of the reporting date, which means that the accumulated depreciation shown is on a life-to-date basis. This report does not show depreciation for the current year separately from prior year amounts, nor can it show the different depreciation types separately (i.e., ordinary depreciation vs. unplanned depreciation vs. special depreciation, etc.).

Also, by default, the amounts shown are planned depreciation amounts for the year and do not take into account whether any depreciation has already been posted in the system. For a report that shows posted values, see Section 2.2.

The Asset Balances report is a simple yet handy report thanks to its self-explanatory display. It is very useful to get a quick snapshot of your asset base as of the reporting date.

▶ Menu Path
Accounting • Financial Accounting • Fixed Assets •
Information System • Reports on Asset Accounting • Preparations for closing • International •
Asset Portfolio (Current Book Values)
▶ Transaction Code
S_ALR_87012041
▶ Technical Report Name
RABEST_ALV01

Main Report Purpose and Recipients

The Asset Portfolio report is the same report as the Asset Balances report (a simple asset listing with acquisition cost, life-to-date depreciation, and net book value) but with posted (as opposed to planned) values. It's used mainly for reconciliation purposes with the General Ledger. The main recipient for this report is the general asset and financial accounting department.

Current Book Value

The option **Current book value** in the **Further settings** section is an important reporting feature because

Asset Balances

Asset	SNo.	Cap.date	Asset description	Σ	Acquis.val.	Σ	Accum.dep.	Σ	Book val.	Crcy
1105	0	11/01/1993	Distribution center Seattle		850,369.00		254,112.00-		596,257.00	USD
1106	0	01/01/1993	Administration Building, Los Angeles		31,888,830.00		9,528,878.00-		22,359,952.00	USD
1107	0	12/05/1994	Sales Office South		773,250.00		202,334.00-		570,916.00	USD
1109	0	01/01/1995	Extension Loading Ramp South		126,000.00		32,760.00-		93,240.00	USD
1111	0	12/31/1996	Administration Building II, Los Angeles		86,687.92		19,146.92-		67,541.00	USD
1112	0	01/01/1993	Production Building 1, New York Plant		996.56		229.56-		767.00	USD
1113	0	01/01/1993	Assembly Building, New York Plant		3,188,883.00		952,892.00-		2,235,991.00	USD
1114	0	03/01/1993	Production Building, Chicago Plant		2,125,922.00		635,266.00-		1,490,656.00	USD
1115	0	10/01/1993	Production Building, Atlanta Plant		2,551,106.00		762,322.00-		1,788,784.00	USD
Company Code 3000				▪	41,592,044.48	▪	12,387,940.48-	▪	29,204,104.00	USD

Figure 2.2 Asset Balances Report – Default Report Layout

it controls what type of depreciation values are shown on the report: planned or posted amounts. By default, most Asset Accounting reports show the planned depreciation amounts and do not take into account whether any depreciation posting runs have been performed yet. Selecting the option **Current book value**, as shown in Figure 2.3 on the other hand, will take posted depreciation amounts into account.

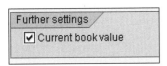

Figure 2.3 The Current Book Value Option

Differences Between the Asset Portfolio and the Asset Balances Reports

To explain how the Asset Portfolio report differs from the Asset Balances report, consider the following example. An asset is capitalized at the beginning of the year. The system has calculated $12,000 planned depreciation for the entire fiscal year ($1,000 per month). Running the Asset Balances report for this asset as of 12/31 would show $12,000 in the **depreciation** column (because this is the planned amount for the entire year). The Asset Portfolio report, however, would show zero in the **depreciation** column (because no depreciation has been posted yet). After the first depreciation posting at the end of January, the Asset Portfolio report would show $1,000 of posted depreciation as of 01/31.

Reconciliation with the General Ledger

The main reason for using this report is for reconciliation purposes with the General Ledger (G/L). For example, run the Asset Portfolio report with a sort version that includes the asset's G/L cost account (i.e., standard sort version 0003) and select the option **Group totals only**,

and you should get a report that looks like the one shown in Figure 2.4.

As you can see, the report shows a subtotal for each G/L account; for example, G/L account **21000 (Office Equipment)** shows an acquisition cost of **$25,000**. To reconcile this amount to the General Ledger, you could simply go to Transaction **FS10N (Display G/L Account Balances)** and compare the account balance to the reported amount in the Asset Portfolio report.

2.3 Total Depreciation Report

The *Total Depreciation* report is much more powerful than the Asset Balances report, because it includes more detailed information about each asset master record as well as the asset's values. It is also a significant report due to its extensive master record field list and corresponding asset values, including beginning and ending balances, current year depreciation, and asset activity summary amounts. In addition, the report provides a great basis as an asset extract tool.

The information required to access the Total Depreciation report is as follows:

▶ **Menu Path**
Accounting • Financial Accounting • Fixed Assets • Information System • Reports on Asset Accounting • Explanations for P&L • International • Depreciation • Total Depreciation

▶ **Transaction Code**
S_ALR_87012004

▶ **Technical Report Name**
RAHAFA_ALV01

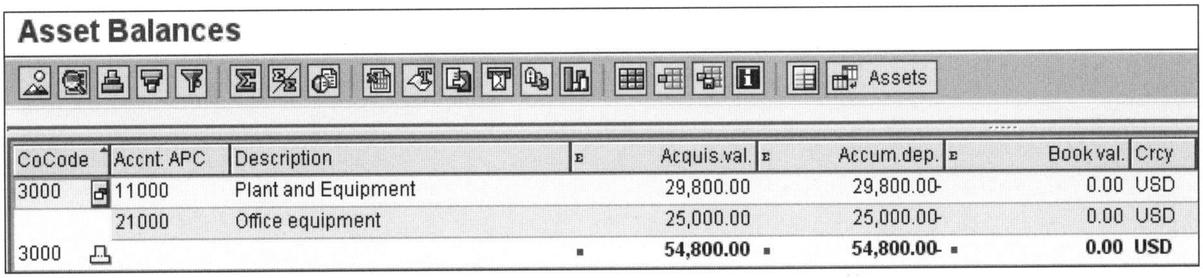

Asset Balances

CoCode	Accnt: APC	Description	Σ	Acquis.val.	Σ	Accum.dep.	Σ	Book val.	Crcy
3000	11000	Plant and Equipment		29,800.00		29,800.00-		0.00	USD
	21000	Office equipment		25,000.00		25,000.00-		0.00	USD
3000			▪	54,800.00	▪	54,800.00-	▪	0.00	USD

Figure 2.4 Asset Balances Sorted and Subtotaled by G/L Account

Main Report Purpose and Recipients

The Total Depreciation report provides an extensive asset listing with beginning and ending balances and detailed information for accumulated depreciation versus current year depreciation. Also, the report can show different depreciation types (ordinary depreciation, unplanned, special, etc.) and it includes a long list of asset master record fields.

This complex report provides a very complete asset-reporting picture because of the breakout of current year depreciation amounts. The main recipients of this report include general asset and financial accounting departments, as well as tax departments (specifically for current year depreciation amounts).

The Selection Screen

The selection screen for this report is almost identical to the basic selection screen discussed in Chapter 1. There are, however, a few small yet important differences in the **Further selections** and **Further settings** sections, as you'll see.

Depreciation Key

The **Further selections** section shown in Figure 2.5 includes a field for the **Depreciation key**. This is a very useful selection criterion that, unfortunately, is missing from the basic selection screen. It allows you to run a report limited to certain depreciation keys only (e.g., it would be easy to limit the report to all non-depreciation assets, or all assets with bonus depreciation keys, etc.).

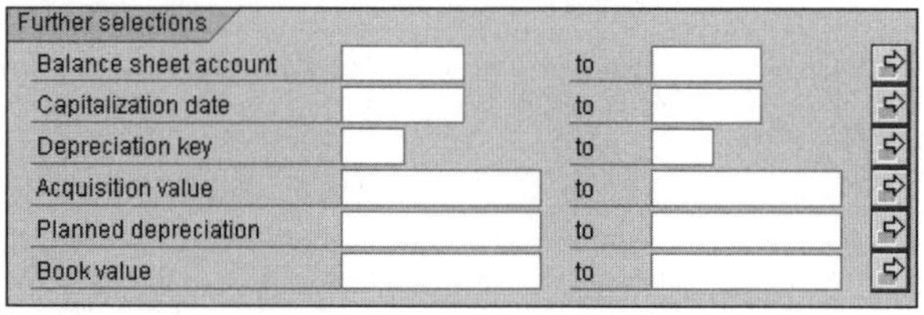

Figure 2.5 Total Depreciation Report Selection Screen – Further Selections

Simulation Version

In addition, the **Further settings** section contains a field for the **Simulation version** (which we will discuss in detail in Chapter 8) and a selection option labeled **Display special dep. separately** (see Figure 2.6). When this option is selected, the report will list the depreciation amounts by

depreciation type. In other words, it will show ordinary depreciation, unplanned depreciation, and special depreciation in separate columns.

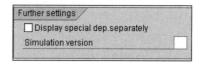

Figure 2.6 Further Settings – Display Option

Ordinary, Unplanned, and Special Depreciation

Before we move on, let's differentiate the depreciation types, as shown in Table 2.1:

Depreciation Type	Description
Ordinary Depreciation	This is the regularly planned depreciation amount for wear and tear during an asset's life.
Unplanned Depreciation	This is depreciation for wear and tear that goes beyond the normal use of an asset. It is in addition to the ordinary depreciation amount and is posted manually by a user. An example of unplanned depreciation could be damage to a company car caused by a severe hail storm.
Special Depreciation	Special depreciation usually pertains to tax depreciation areas and is in addition to ordinary depreciation. An example of special depreciation is the *US Bonus depreciation* that was implemented for the year 2001–2004.

Table 2.1 Different Depreciation Types

The Total Depreciation report shows the beginning of the year values for the assets, as well as the ending balances as of the report date. Beginning/Ending values include asset cost, depreciation, and net book value. Figure 2.7 shows the three columns for the beginning of the year values.

Cum.acq.value	Accum.dep.	Start book.val
850,369.00	237,104.00-	613,265.00
31,888,830.00	8,891,101.00-	22,997,729.00
773,250.00	186,869.00-	586,381.00

Figure 2.7 Beginning of the Year Values

In between these values, the report shows current year depreciation (again, the report can list depreciation by depreciation type (ordinary, unplanned, special) when the **Display special dep. separately** option is selected).

This very useful feature is commonly used by accounting and tax departments to report and reconcile depreciation amounts for the current fiscal year. Figure 2.8 shows the planned depreciation amounts for the current fiscal year by depreciation type.

Σ	Plnd.ODep	Σ	Pld.unpl.dep.	Σ	Plnd.SDep
	53,149.00-		0.00		0.00
	17,008.00-		0.00		0.00
	637,777.00-		0.00		0.00

Figure 2.8 Planned Depreciation Amounts by Depreciation Type

Sum of Current Year Activity

In addition, the Total Depreciation report includes several columns to show the sum of all current year activity. Current year activity includes all asset postings that occurred during the year (e.g., asset acquisitions, retirements, transfers, etc.). Figure 2.9 shows the columns for these transactional values.

Σ Trans.acq.val	Σ Trns.AccDep	Σ Trns.ord.dep.	Σ Trns.spec.dep.	Σ Trns.unpl.dep.
5,500.00	0.00	0.00	0.00	0.00
248,317.00	0.00	0.00	0.00	0.00
67,000.00	0.00	0.00	0.00	0.00

Figure 2.9 Sum of All Transactional Values for the Fiscal Year

These value columns have caused quite a bit of confusion for companies in the past, so we'll look at them in detail in Table 2.2.

Asset Fields

Unlike the Asset Balances report, the Total Depreciation report includes a long list of asset fields by default, which is another reason why this report is so useful. Below is a list of fields that are included in the basic version of this report:

▸ **General Asset Information**
  ▸ Company Code
  ▸ Asset Main Number and Subnumber
  ▸ Capitalization Date
  ▸ Description
  ▸ Quantity and Unit of Measure
▸ **Time-Dependent Asset Information**
  ▸ Plant
  ▸ Cost Center
  ▸ WBS (Work Breakdown Structure) Element
  ▸ Location
  ▸ Vendor

Column	Description
Beginning Balances	
Cum.acq.value	Accumulated acquisition cost for an asset
Accum.dep.	Accumulated depreciation (includes accumulated ordinary, unplanned, special and transfer of reserves depreciation amounts)
Cum.O.dep.	Accumulated ordinary depreciation
Cum.S.dep.	Accumulated special depreciation
Cum.unpl.dep.	Accumulated unplanned depreciation
Cum.trns.res.	Accumulated transfers of reserves depreciation
Start book.val	Starting book value at the beginning of the year
Planned Depreciation	
PlndDep	Planned depreciation (includes ordinary, unplanned, special and transfer of reserves depreciation amounts)
Plnd.ODep	Planned ordinary depreciation amounts for the reporting period
Plnd.SDep	Planned special depreciation amounts for the reporting period
Pld.unpl.dep	Planned unplanned depreciation amounts for the reporting period
Plnd.trns.res	Planned transfer of reserves depreciation amounts for the reporting period
Transactions (for the reporting period)	
Trans.acq.val	Sum of the acquisition values for all transactions during the reporting period (includes asset acquisitions, retirements, transfers, etc.)
Trns.AccDep	Sum of the accumulated depreciation values for all transactions (includes accumulated ordinary, unplanned, special and transfer of reserves depreciation amounts)
Trns.ord.dep.	Sum of the ordinary depreciation values for all transactions
Trns.spec.dep.	Sum of the special depreciation values for all transactions
Trns.unpl.dep.	Sum of the unplanned depreciation values for all transactions
Trns.manl.dep.	Sum of the manual depreciation values for all transactions
Write-ups	Write-up postings (to offset overdepreciation)
Ending Balances	
End book val	Ending book value as of the reporting date

Table 2.2 Transactional Value Columns

▶ **Depreciation Terms**
  ▶ Depreciation Key
  ▶ Useful Life
  ▶ Depreciation Start Date (ordinary depreciation start date and special depreciation start date)

Adding Fields to the Total Depreciation Report

Figure 2.10 shows the Total Depreciation report in its default layout, sorted and sub-totaled by company code (standard sort version 0013). As you can tell, many fields are hidden but could be added to the report output by clicking the **Change Layout** icon (Ctrl + F8).

To include additional fields in this report, you should use the appropriate sort versions. For example, to add the asset **Class** field to this report, simply use a sort version that includes the asset **Class** field as a sort/subtotal level (i.e., standard Asset Accounting sort version 0007).

Figure 2.11 shows how the report changes when using sort version 0007. The report now shows the asset **Class** field and added subtotals for each asset class. If you're unclear about how this works (i.e., regarding the importance of choosing the correct sort version), read Section 1.5.

Extracting Asset Information

Because this report includes so many asset master record fields and asset values, it's a great choice as an asset extract tool. If, for example, you need to extract asset information for further processing (i.e., for input into a

third-party property tax system, or an inventory management system, etc.) consider using the Total Depreciation report. You can download it easily into Excel in a single-line format just by clicking the **Local File** icon (F9).

2.4 Posted Depreciation Reports

The standard Asset Accounting information system offers two different reports for posted depreciation. The first report lists posted depreciation amounts by asset number and posting period, while the second report lists posted depreciation by cost centers.

Posted Depreciation by Asset and Posting Period Report

The *Posted Depreciation by Asset and Posting Period* report shows the actual posted depreciation (as opposed to planned depreciation amounts) for each individual asset record and by posting period.

The information required to access the Posted Depreciation by Asset and Posting Period report is as follows:

▶ **Menu Path**
Accounting • Financial Accounting • Fixed Assets • Information System • Reports on Asset Accounting • Cost Accounting • Depreciation Posted • Posted depreciation by asset and posting period

CoCd	Asset	SNo.	Cap.date	Asset description	Plant	Cost Ctr	Locati	DepKy	Life	Ord.dep.Start	Σ Cum.acq.value	Σ Accum.dep.	Σ Start book.v	Σ Plnd.ODep	Σ Plnd.SDe
3000	1100	0	01/01/1993	Production Building 1, New York Plant	3000	1000	1	LINB	050/000	01/01/1993	2,657,403.00	740,937.00-	1,916,466.00	53,149.00-	0.0
	1105	0	11/01/1993	Distribution center Seattle	3400	1000	1	LINB	050/000	11/01/1993	850,369.00	237,104.00-	613,265.00	17,008.00-	0.0
	1106	0	01/01/1993	Administration Building, Los Angeles	3300	1000	1	LINB	050/000	01/01/1993	31,888,830.00	8,891,101.00-	22,997,729....	637,777.00-	0.0

Figure 2.10 Total Depreciation Report – Default Layout

CoCd	Class	Asset	SNo.	Cap.date	Asset description	Plant	Cost Ctr	Locati	DepKy	Life	Ord.dep.Start	Σ Cum.acq.value	Σ Accum.dep.	Σ Start book.val	Σ Plnd.ODep
3000	1000	1118	0	01/01/1993	Plant site, Los Angeles	3300	4290	1	0000	000/000	01/01/1993	15,667,260.00	0.00	15,667,260.00	0.00
		1119	0	10/01/1993	Plant site, Atlanta	3200	4275	1	0000	000/000	10/01/1993	7,833,630.00	0.00	7,833,630.00	0.00
	1000											▪ 23,500,890.00	▪ 0.00	▪ 23,500,890.00	▪ 0.00
	1100	1100	0	01/01/1993	Production Building 1, New York Plant	3000	1000	1	LINB	050/000	01/01/1993	2,657,403.00	740,937.00-	1,916,466.00	53,149.00-
		1105	0	11/01/1993	Distribution center Seattle	3400	1000	1	LINB	050/000	11/01/1993	850,369.00	237,104.00-	613,265.00	17,008.00-
	1100											▪ 3,507,772.00	▪ 978,041.00-	▪ 2,529,731.00	▪ 70,157.00-
3000												▪▪ 27,008,662.00	▪▪ 978,041.00-	▪▪ 26,030,621.00	▪▪ 70,157.00-

Figure 2.11 Total Depreciation Report, Including Subtotal by Asset Clas

▶ **Transaction Code**
  S_P99_41000192
▶ **Technical Report Name**
  Query – AM28

Main Report Purpose and Recipients

This report lists the actual depreciation that was posted to the individual asset master records for each depreciation period. The report lists the different depreciation types (ordinary, special, unplanned, etc.) in separate columns. The main recipients of the report are the general financial and asset accounting departments.

The Selection Screen

Figure 2.12 shows that the selection screen for this report is very different from the basic selection screen. The only available selection criteria are the **Company Code**, **Asset Number**, **Sub-Number**, **Cost Center**, and depreciation posting year and period. None of the standard selection options, including the dynamic selections, are available. Furthermore, you cannot enter a sort version on the selection screen. This limits the usability of this report significantly.

Report Output

Figure 2.13 shows the default report output. As you can see, this report breaks out the depreciation amounts by depreciation type (ordinary, unplanned, special, etc.) and

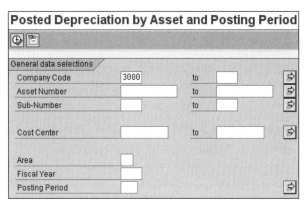

Figure 2.12 Posted Depreciation Report – Selection Screen

shows the posted amounts for each period. No other information is included in this report. Furthermore, you cannot add any fields to this report as you could with the Asset Balances report or the Total Depreciation report.

The report does not let users specify a sort version on the selection screen; however, because this report is Advanced List Viewer (ALV) enabled, you can still sort and subtotal it after it has been executed. For example, Figure 2.14 shows the exact same report, except for the fact that it is sorted and subtotaled by the posting period (**Per.**) field.

Although this report seems limited in its functionality and scope, it is still very useful. Its main purpose is the reconciliation of overall posted depreciation amounts for a specific posting period, between the asset sub-ledger and the General Ledger.

Posted Depreciation by Asset and Posting Period

Posted Depreciation by Asset and Posting Period

Asset	Sub-number	Per.	Ordinary depreciat.	Currency	Unplanned depr.	Currency	Special depr.	Currency	Interest	Currency	Reserves transf.	Currency
1100	0	001	4,429.00-	USD	0.00	USD	0.00	USD	0.00	USD	0.00	USD
		002	4,430.00-	USD	0.00	USD	0.00	USD	0.00	USD	0.00	USD
		003	4,429.00-	USD	0.00	USD	0.00	USD	0.00	USD	0.00	USD
1105		001	1,418.00-	USD	0.00	USD	0.00	USD	0.00	USD	0.00	USD
		002	1,417.00-	USD	0.00	USD	0.00	USD	0.00	USD	0.00	USD
		003	1,417.00-	USD	0.00	USD	0.00	USD	0.00	USD	0.00	USD
1106		001	53,149.00-	USD	0.00	USD	0.00	USD	0.00	USD	0.00	USD
		002	53,148.00-	USD	0.00	USD	0.00	USD	0.00	USD	0.00	USD
		003	53,148.00-	USD	0.00	USD	0.00	USD	0.00	USD	0.00	USD
Company code 3000			176,985.00-	USD	0.00	USD	0.00	USD	0.00	USD	0.00	USD
			176,985.00-	USD	0.00	USD	0.00	USD	0.00	USD	0.00	USD

Figure 2.13 Posted Depreciation Report – Default Report Layout

Posted Depreciation by Asset and Posting Period

Posted Depreciation by Asset and Posting Period

Asset	Sub-number	Per.	¤ Ordinary depreciat.	Currency	¤ Unplanned depr.	Currency	¤ Special de...	Currency	¤ Interest	Currency	¤ Reserves transf.	Currency
1100	0	001	4,429.00-	USD	0.00	USD	0.00	USD	0.00	USD	0.00	USD
1105	0		1,418.00-	USD	0.00	USD	0.00	USD	0.00	USD	0.00	USD
1106	0		53,149.00-	USD	0.00	USD	0.00	USD	0.00	USD	0.00	USD
		⚏ 001 ▪	58,996.00- USD		▪ 0.00 USD		▪ 0.00 USD		▪ 0.00 USD		▪ 0.00 USD	
1100	0	002	4,430.00-	USD	0.00	USD	0.00	USD	0.00	USD	0.00	USD
1105	0		1,417.00-	USD	0.00	USD	0.00	USD	0.00	USD	0.00	USD
1106	0		53,148.00-	USD	0.00	USD	0.00	USD	0.00	USD	0.00	USD
		⚏ 002 ▪	58,995.00- USD		▪ 0.00 USD		▪ 0.00 USD		▪ 0.00 USD		▪ 0.00 USD	
1100	0	003	4,429.00-	USD	0.00	USD	0.00	USD	0.00	USD	0.00	USD
1105	0		1,417.00-	USD	0.00	USD	0.00	USD	0.00	USD	0.00	USD
1106	0		53,148.00-	USD	0.00	USD	0.00	USD	0.00	USD	0.00	USD
		⚏ 003 ▪	58,994.00- USD		▪ 0.00 USD		▪ 0.00 USD		▪ 0.00 USD		▪ 0.00 USD	
⚏		▪ ▪	176,985.00- USD		▪ ▪ 0.00 USD		▪ ▪ 0.00 USD		▪ ▪ 0.00 USD		▪ ▪ 0.00 USD	

Figure 2.14 Posted Depreciation Report – Sorted and Subtotaled by Period

Posted Depreciation Related to Cost Centers Report

Just like the Posted Depreciation by Asset and Posting Period report, the *Posted Depreciation Related to Cost Centers* report lists the posted depreciation (broken out by depreciation type) for each individual asset and posting period. In fact, the two reports share the same selection screen. In addition, this report shows which cost center the depreciation was posted to.

The information required to access the Posted Depreciation Related to Cost Centers report is as follows:

> ▶ **Menu Path**
> **Accounting • Financial Accounting • Fixed Assets • Information System • Reports on Asset Accounting • Cost Accounting • Depreciation Posted • Posted depreciation, related to cost centers**
> ▶ **Transaction Code**
> **S_P99_87010175**
> ▶ **Technical Report Name**
> **Query – AM27**

Main Report Purpose and Recipients

This report lists the actual depreciation that was posted to the cost center of the individual asset master records for each depreciation period. The report lists the different depreciation types (ordinary, special, unplanned, etc.) in separate columns. The main recipients of this report are the general financial and asset accounting departments, and cost center and department managers.

Report Output

Figure 2.15 shows the default report output. It is important to note that the cost center shown in this report is the cost center where depreciation was posted to and not necessarily the current cost center of an asset. For example, in Figure 2.15, **Asset** number **1105** is listed on the report under **Cost center 1000**. This was the cost center that the asset was assigned to in January of 2006 (reporting date), but it could be assigned to a different cost center today.

The main reason for using this report is therefore to support cost center managers or department heads with monthly financial information.

2.5 Depreciation Forecast Report (Depreciation Simulation)

The *Depreciation Forecast* report (also known as the *Depreciation Simulation* report) can be used to produce very accurate depreciation forecasts for existing assets, as well as planned and existing capital investments (such as appropriation requests, investment management program positions, internal orders, and Work Breakdown Structures (WBS) elements).

Posted depreciation, related to cost centers

Posted depreciation, related to cost centers

CoCd	Cost center	Per.	Asset	Sub-number	Σ Ordinary depreciat.	Currency	Σ Special depr.	Currency	Σ Unplanned depr.	Currency	Σ Reserves transf.	Currency	Σ Interest rates	Currency
3000	1000	001	1100	0	4,429.00-	USD	0.00	USD	0.00	USD	0.00	USD	0.00	USD
			1105	0	1,418.00-	USD	0.00	USD	0.00	USD	0.00	USD	0.00	USD
			1106	0	53,149.00-	USD	0.00	USD	0.00	USD	0.00	USD	0.00	USD
		001			58,996.00- USD		0.00 USD		0.00 USD		0.00 USD		0.00 USD	
		002	1100	0	4,430.00-	USD	0.00	USD	0.00	USD	0.00	USD	0.00	USD
			1105	0	1,417.00-	USD	0.00	USD	0.00	USD	0.00	USD	0.00	USD
			1106	0	53,148.00-	USD	0.00	USD	0.00	USD	0.00	USD	0.00	USD
		002			58,995.00- USD		0.00 USD		0.00 USD		0.00 USD		0.00 USD	
		003	1100	0	4,429.00-	USD	0.00	USD	0.00	USD	0.00	USD	0.00	USD
			1105	0	1,417.00-	USD	0.00	USD	0.00	USD	0.00	USD	0.00	USD
			1106	0	53,148.00-	USD	0.00	USD	0.00	USD	0.00	USD	0.00	USD
		003			58,994.00- USD		0.00 USD		0.00 USD		0.00 USD		0.00 USD	
	1000				176,985.00- USD		0.00 USD		0.00 USD		0.00 USD		0.00 USD	
3000					176,985.00- USD		0.00 USD		0.00 USD		0.00 USD		0.00 USD	
					176,985.00- USD		0.00 USD		0.00 USD		0.00 USD		0.00 USD	

Figure 2.15 Posted Depreciation, Related to Cost Centers Report

The information required to access the Depreciation Forecast report is as follows:

> ▶ **Menu Path**
> **Accounting • Financial Accounting • Fixed Assets • Information System • Reports on Asset Accounting • Depreciation Forecast • Depreciation on Capitalized Assets (Depreciation Simulation)**
> ▶ **Transaction Code**
> **S_ALR_87012936**
> ▶ **Technical Report Name**
> **RASIMU02**

Main Report Purpose and Recipients

This is a very complex report used to forecast depreciation amounts for existing assets, as well as existing and planned capital investment measures. Forecast can be for multiple reporting periods and years. The main recipients for this report are the general asset accounting department, tax department, cost center, and department and other budget managers.

Actual Year-End Depreciation Amounts

First, let's identify what determines the actual depreciation amounts at the end of any given fiscal year. Actual depreciation is the result of four components and the system can forecast depreciation for most of these components very accurately:

▶ Depreciation for existing fixed assets
▶ Depreciation related to existing capital investment measures (internal orders and WBS elements)
▶ Depreciation expected for planned capital investments (appropriation requests)
▶ Depreciation adjustments for asset activity such as retirements and transfers

Let's look at each of these components in more detail.

Depreciation for existing fixed assets
For existing fixed assets, the system can calculate depreciation amounts to the penny because it has all the required information for such a calculation (i.e., acquisition cost, net book value, depreciation method, useful life, depreciation start date, etc.).

Depreciation related to existing capital investment measures
Depreciation for existing investment measures (such as internal orders or WBS elements) can be calculated fairly accurately, if the depreciation simulation data has been maintained in the master records of the internal orders and WBS elements.

Figure 2.16 shows the details of the **Depreciation simulation data** section of an internal order. Notice that you can specify asset classes (from which the system can derive depreciation methods and useful lives) and estimated in-service dates (or capitalization dates). With this information, the system can now calculate an estimated depreciation amount based on the planned or budgeted amount of the investment measure.

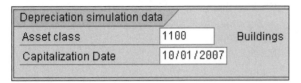

Figure 2.16 Depreciation Simulation Data of an Internal Order

Depreciation expected for planned capital investments
The same logic applies to planned investments, which are usually represented by *Appropriation Requests* (AR) in SAP. The AR master record has a depreciation simulation screen, too, and you can enter the same depreciation simulation data as before (see Figure 2.17).

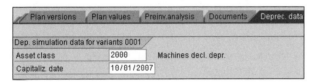

Figure 2.17 Depreciation Simulation Data of an Appropriation Request

Another important feature of this report is its ability to forecast depreciation for existing capital investment measures (internal orders or WBS elements) either based on planned amounts or budgeted amounts. See Figure 2.18 for the corresponding setting on the report's selection screen. By default, all depreciation forecast amounts for capital investment measures are based on the planned amounts.

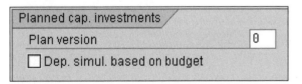

Figure 2.18 Depreciation Simulation Based on Planned or Budgeted Amounts

Depreciation adjustments for asset activity
The only component that the system cannot possibly forecast depreciation for is the on-going activity throughout the year, such as asset retirements or asset trans-

fers. Forecasting this kind of asset activity is difficult, and therefore any depreciation forecast cannot be 100 percent accurate. Nevertheless, the asset master record contains a planned retirement date (**Plnd. retirement on**) field that, when filled out, will be considered during the depreciation forecast (see Figure 2.19).

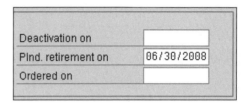

Figure 2.19 Planned Retirement Date on Asset Master Record

For example, if you entered 6/30/2008 as the planned retirement date for an asset, the Depreciation Simulation report would forecast depreciation only up to this date, as long as the **Sim. only to planned retmt.** option in the **Further settings** section is checked (see Figure 2.20).

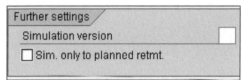

Figure 2.20 Simulation Only Until Planned Retirement

All things considered, depreciation forecasts in Asset Accounting can be very accurate, as long as the appropriate depreciation simulation data and planned retirement dates in the corresponding master records are maintained.

The Selection Screen
The standard Depreciation Simulation report uses a modified selection screen as shown in Figure 2.21. It allows users to include or exclude each depreciation-producing group of objects (e.g., existing assets, internal orders, WBS elements, and appropriation requests).

To include the existing assets in the depreciation forecast, make sure to select the **Select assets** option. To include existing and planned capital investment measures, select the corresponding options in the screen section labeled **Planned cap. investments**.

To produce a depreciation forecast for multiple years, simply enter a report date in the future. For example, if you wanted to produce a five-year forecast (starting with the current year, i.e., 2007), you would enter 12/31/2011 as the report date (assuming that your fiscal year is a standard calendar year).

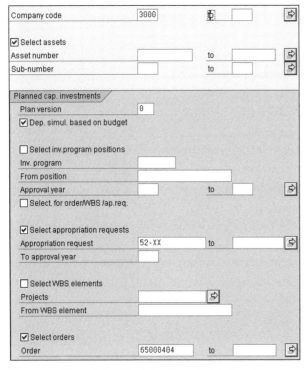

Figure 2.21 Depreciation Simulation Report – Selection Screen

Evaluation Period

Additionally, the selection screen contains a section labeled **Evaluation period**, which tells the report to out-

put annual, quarterly, semi-annual, or monthly values (see Figure 2.22). This makes it possible to use this report for monthly depreciation forecasts for the current year, quarterly forecasts for the next two years, or even annual forecasts for the next five years.

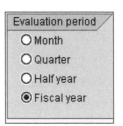

Figure 2.22 Evaluation Period

Report Output

When you put it all together, a good example of a three-year annual depreciation forecast or simulation looks like the one shown in Figure 2.23.

Unlike the Depreciation Forecast report in older SAP releases (prior to 4.7), this report produces a horizontal forecast (as opposed to the former reports' vertical forecast output). This display makes it much easier to work with the information. Moreover, the new Depreciation Forecast report is ALV-enabled and downloads easily into Microsoft Excel.

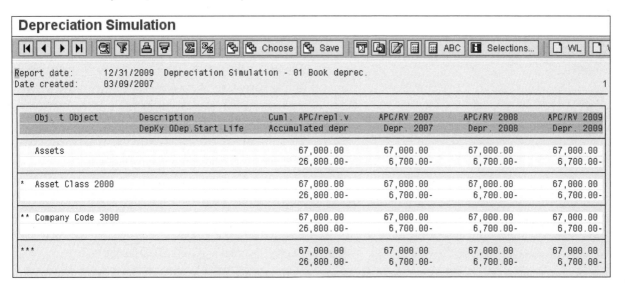

Figure 2.23 Annual Depreciation Simulation for Three Years

Caveats

The only two complaints I have regarding the Depreciation Forecast report are that the selection screen doesn't allow you to enter a sort version, and the maximum forecast range is only 12 years.

2.6 Chapter Summary

In this chapter, you learned about the most important balance-based asset reports. After reading this chapter, you should have a good understanding of the main reports used to show asset balances. The reports to remember from this chapter are:

▶ **Asset Balances**

This is a simple yet very useful asset listing, which includes the asset cost, life-to-date depreciation, and net book value as of the reporting date. All values are planned amounts as opposed to posted amounts.

▶ **Asset Portfolio**

This report is the same as the Asset Balances report, except for the fact that it shows posted amounts instead of planned amounts. This makes it an ideal reconciliation report.

▶ **Total Depreciation**

This is a very powerful report that shows beginning and ending balances, as well as prior year versus current year depreciation amounts by depreciation type (ordinary, unplanned, special depreciation). You should use this report as one of your main asset reports.

▶ **Posted Depreciation**

Two reports are available to show the posted depreciation amounts (posted depreciation by period or posted depreciation by cost centers). Both reports are useful when reconciling monthly posting values or cost center postings.

▶ **Depreciation Simulation**

This report is a very complex and powerful forecasting report, which can accurately predict depreciation expense for existing fixed assets, as well as planned and existing capital investments (via the use of depreciation simulation data for appropriation requests, WBS elements, and internal orders).

There are, of course, many more balance-based asset reports, especially versions tailored to specific countries. This list, however, gives you the details for the most commonly used reports for reporting asset balances.

Looking ahead, in Chapter 3, you will learn all about the most important transaction-based asset reports.

3 Transaction Reports

Many different transactions can occur during an asset's life. Such transactions include acquisition postings, retirements, transfers, and various other adjustments. This chapter details the most commonly used asset transaction reports and discusses their features, intended use, and recipients.

3.1 The Hierarchical Nature of Transaction Reports

Transaction reports are hierarchical in nature. This means that each report has the following:

▶ A main level (usually the asset level)

▶ A subhierarchy below it (usually the actual transactions)

For example, Figure 3.1 shows a screenshot of an asset transaction report. Notice asset number **2187-0** and the corresponding four transactions listed below it. As you can see, the report summarizes all transactions for this asset on the asset level itself and shows the individual transaction amounts below the asset.

You should also note the double-triangle icon in front of the word **Asset** in the upper left portion of the report. Clicking on this icon allows you to open or close the transaction detail for this asset. In other words, it allows you to view the report in a detailed version (listing individual transaction detail) like Figure 3.1 or in a summarized version (summary of all transactions on the asset level) as shown in Figure 3.2.

| Asset | SNo. | Cap.date | Asset description | | | APC | Val. adjustmt | Dep. on trans. |
| DocumentNo | Pstng Date | TType | Ast.val.dt | Reference | Quantity BUn | APC | Val. adjustmt | Dep. on trans. Crcy |
		Text						
2187	0	09/30/2002	Transmitter			38,470.00	0.00	1,124.00-
100000376	09/30/2002	115	09/30/2002			1,220.00	0.00	36.00- USD
		ORD 812403						
100000377	09/30/2002	115	09/30/2002			19,600.00	0.00	572.00- USD
		ORD 812402						
100000378	09/30/2002	115	09/30/2002			6,600.00	0.00	193.00- USD
		ORD 812404						
100000379	09/30/2002	115	09/30/2002			11,050.00	0.00	323.00- USD
		ORD 812405						

Figure 3.1 Asset Transaction Report – Detailed Version

| Asset | SNo. | Cap.date | Asset description | | | APC | Val. adjustmt | Dep. on trans. |
| DocumentNo | Pstng Date | TType | Ast.val.dt | Reference | Quantity BUn | APC | Val. adjustmt | Dep. on trans. Crcy |
		Text						
2187	0	09/30/2002	Transmitter			38,470.00	0.00	1,124.00-
2188	0	09/19/2002	Equipment with Bonus Depreciation			15,000.00	0.00	438.00-
2189	0	09/19/2002	Equipment without Bonus Depreciation			15,000.00	0.00	438.00-
2190	0	09/19/2002	Test Equipment with Bonus Depreciation			25,000.00	0.00	730.00-

Figure 3.2 Asset Transaction Report – Summary Version

The Downside of Hierarchical Reports

While having this level of detail in hierarchical reports is a great feature, it unfortunately comes with a downside. The Advanced List Viewer (ALV) does not fully support hierarchical reports. Consequently, certain layout features that are available for balance-based reports are not offered for transaction-based reports.

Specifically, the direct integration with Microsoft Excel or Microsoft Word is not available (but the download function still is available). The **ABC Analysis** and **SAP Graphics** options are also unavailable. For example, if you tried to run a hierarchical list report (such as the Asset Transaction report) with the **List assets** setting, the system issues error message **AB063 - Use of ALV grid not supported for hierarchical lists**.

The irony here is that the **Display** option **Use ALV grid** is still available on the selection screen of transaction reports. But, in order to use it, you have to use the **...or group totals only** setting. Again, trying to run a transaction report with asset detail and ALV will result in error message AB063.

3.2 Asset Acquisitions Report

The *Asset Acquisitions* report lists all acquisition transactions for the specified posting date time period. This is quite an interesting feature because it allows you to run this report for mid-year time intervals (i.e. run it for all acquisitions that were posted in the second fiscal quarter). Many other Asset Accounting reports are limited to a year-to-date time period instead.

The information required to access the Asset Acquisitions report is as follows:

▸ **Menu Path**
Accounting • Financial Accounting • Fixed Assets • Information System • Reports on Asset Accounting • Day-to-Day Activities • International • Asset Acquisitions
▸ **Transaction Code**
S_ALR_87012050
▸ **Technical Report Name**
RAZUGA_ALV01

Main Report Purpose and Recipients

This report lists all acquisition transactions for the specified posting period. Amounts shown include acquisition cost and corresponding depreciation amounts as well as detailed information for each individual transaction (such as posting date, document number, etc.). The main recipients for this report are general asset accounting departments, and also tax departments.

Caution

You'll have to consider different accounting standards when it comes to asset acquisitions! Different countries have different definitions for asset acquisitions – more information to follow.

Hierarchical Asset Display

Because an asset can have multiple acquisition transactions in the posting date time period that is specified for the report, the report creates a hierarchical display by listing the main asset record information (with summary values of all transactions on the main level and all individual transaction detail on the sub-level). Figure 3.3 shows the standard report layout for the Asset Acquisitions report. Notice that asset number **2219-0** shows a total acquisi-

Asset	SNo.	Cap.date	Asset description		Acquisition	O.dep.	S.dep.	Crcy
	DocumentNo	Pstng Date	TType Ast.val.dt Reference	Quantity BUn	Acquisition	O.dep.	S.dep.	Crcy
		Text						
2219	0	10/31/2002	Transmitter		66,100.00	1,378.00-	0.00	USD
	100000385	10/31/2002	115 10/31/2002		48,100.00	1,003.00-	0.00	USD
		ORD 812412						
	100000386	10/31/2002	115 10/31/2002		18,000.00	375.00-	0.00	USD
		ORD 812412						
* Total					66,100.00	1,378.00-	0.00	USD
					66,100.00	1,378.00-	0.00	USD

Figure 3.3 Asset Acquisitions Report – Detailed Version

tion cost of **$66,100.00**, which was posted in two acquisition transactions shown just below the asset level.

The Selection Screen

The selection screen for this report varies slightly from the basic selection screen. It includes the additional selection fields **Transaction type** and **Posting date** in the **Further selections** section (see Figure 3.4).

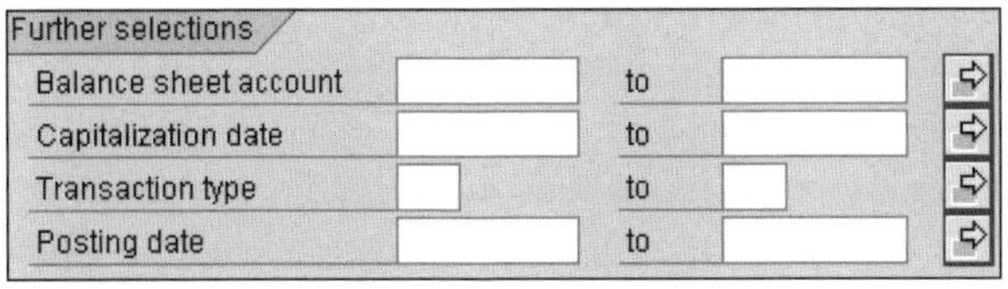

Figure 3.4 Selection Screen – Further Selections

Transaction Types

First, it's important for you to know that all fixed asset transactions must be posted with a transaction type. This is a fairly unique feature of the Asset Accounting module (only the consolidation application uses transactions types, too, albeit different ones). Other modules like Accounts Payable, Accounts Receivable, or the General Ledger don't use these transaction types.

The transaction type is a three-digit code that groups an asset transaction by category, such as acquisitions (default transaction type range 100-199), retirements (200-299), transfers (300-399), and so on for various other categories. Furthermore, the transaction type determines whether a transaction is a debit or credit, whether depreciation should be calculated, or whether the asset should be capitalized or deactivated, as well as many more settings.

The **Transaction type** limitation allows you to narrow down the report to just certain types of acquisitions (e.g., acquisitions from affiliated companies only or goods receipts only).

Using the **Posting date** limitation, you can create an acquisitions report for any time period during the current fiscal year (i.e., month of March, or second fiscal quarter, etc.).

Defining an Asset Acquisition

This is a good time to repeat a caution already cited earlier in this section, namely, the importance of consider-

ing different accounting standards when it comes to asset acquisitions. You might think that an asset acquisition is always an asset acquisition. But, that is not the case. Different countries have different definitions for asset acquisitions. Consider the following scenario.

A Possible Scenario

Say you use internal orders or Work Breakdown Structure (WBS) elements for your asset capitalization process. The process usually starts when someone in your organization requests money to be spent for a capital item (e.g., the purchase and installation of a new server). The request is approved and an internal order or WBS element is created to capture all costs associated with this capital project.

Then, let's say that in December of 2007 you receive the server and an invoice for $10,000. This amount is posted to the internal order. You cannot put the server in service just yet, because you're waiting for the required rack mount; therefore, at the end of December, the internal order is kept open and the spending is settled to an *Asset under Construction* (AuC). By default, the system uses transaction type 114 – 116 (depending on your configuration settings for the default transaction types used in Asset Accounting) to debit the AuC for $10,000.

In January of 2008, you receive the rack mount and corresponding invoice for $2,000, which is posted to the internal order. This item completes the project and the status of the order is changed to technically complete (TECO) or closed (CLSD). At the end of the month, the order is settled to the final asset master record (the installed server).

What's Happening Behind the Scenes

While you may not realize it, the system actually processes this final settlement in three steps:

1. The system settles the $2,000 of current year spending to the AuC using transaction types 114 - 116.
2. The system then transfers $10,000 from the AuC to the final asset using transaction types 338 (credit to the AuC) and 331 (debit to the final asset).
3. Lastly, the system transfers $2,000 from the AuC to the final asset using transaction types 339 (credit to the AuC) and 336 (debit to the final asset).

You would now assume that you've placed in service an asset worth $12,000 in fiscal year 2008, correct? At least that's what the IRS would expect you to show on your acquisition report. However, when you run the Asset Acquisitions report for this scenario, the report would show an acquisition for $2,000 only. The $10,000 that was originally spent in 2007 is considered to be a transfer and would therefore only show up on an Asset Transfers report.

In other words, the standard SAP acquisition report does not consider transaction type 331 an acquisition transaction; instead, this transaction type is considered to be a transfer from a prior year AuC to a final asset in the current year.

This reporting logic is a valid accounting principle in Germany; and because SAP is a German company, it should come as no surprise that the standard acquisition report adheres to this accounting principle.

Entering Specific Transaction Types
What does this mean for your Asset Acquisitions report? Does it render it useless? Hardly. What it comes down to is your asset acquisition process and what you consider to be an acquisition in the various countries in which you might work. For most European countries, the standard SAP logic should be satisfactory, but for the US, this would not be the case.

The solution is quite simple, because the report includes another interesting feature. If you leave the **Transaction type** selection criteria field (see Figure 3.4) blank, the report uses the standard SAP logic as described. If, however, you enter specific transaction types that you consider to be acquisitions, it will show these transactions instead, regardless of what they are.

Caution
If you inadvertently enter a Retirements transaction type (i.e., transaction type 200), the report would show this, too! So, ensure that you pay attention to the transaction type limitations. In general, *transaction types* (TTY) are grouped into the following basic categories:
TTY 100-199: Asset Acquisitions
TTY 200-299: Asset Retirements
TTY 300-399: Asset Transfers

TTY 400-499: Post Capitalizations
TTY 500-599: Depreciation Postings
TTY 600-699: Manual Depreciation
TTY 700-799: Write-up Postings
TTY 800-899: Revaluations
TTY 900-999: Data Takeover Transactions

You should figure out exactly what transactions are considered to be asset acquisitions in the country you work in and then limit the Asset Acquisitions report to just these transactions. Then, save the report as a variant so that you don't have to enter the limitations again when you want to run the report.

3.3 Asset Retirements Report

The *Asset Retirements* report is a comprehensive report for all asset retirements, including asset sale (retirements with revenue) and asset scrap (retirements without revenue). The report shows the cost amounts being retired, corresponding depreciation amounts, resulting gain/loss amounts, and any sales proceeds in case of asset sales.

The information required to access the Asset Retirements report is as follows:

▶ **Menu Path**
  Accounting • Financial Accounting • Fixed Assets • Information System • Reports on Asset Accounting • Day-to-Day Activities • International • Asset Retirements
▶ **Transaction Code**
  S_ALR_87012052
▶ **Technical Report Name**
  RAABGA_ALV01

Main Report Purpose and Recipients
This report is a comprehensive report, which includes retirement amounts (cost and depreciation) and corresponding gain and loss amounts. Also included are sales proceeds in case of an asset sale (as opposed to asset scrap) and statistical subsequent cost or revenues. The main recipients of this report are general asset accounting departments and tax departments.

The Selection Screen

The selection screen for the Asset Retirements report is almost identical to the selection screen of the Asset Acquisitions report. The only difference, that the field **Deactivation date** is an available selection criteria, is shown in Figure 3.5. This allows you to limit this report to a specific time period, during which the assets were deactivated (which may be different from the actual posting date of the retirements).

Further selections					
Balance sheet account		to			⇨
Capitalization date		to			⇨
Deactivation date		to			⇨
Transaction type		to			⇨
Posting date		to			⇨

Figure 3.5 Deactivation Date in Further Selections

Report Output

On the individual transaction level, the Asset Retirements report shows detailed posting information, such as the posting date, transaction type, and document number (see Figure 3.6).

Statistical Subsequent Cost or Revenue Postings

The Asset Retirements report also can show statistical subsequent cost or revenue postings. To explain this, let's go through an example. Assume that you post a simple asset scrap to a piece of machinery in one of your plants. The posting is done in the month of March. Two months later, you receive an invoice from one of your vendors who has de-installed the machine and is now charging you for costs associated with dismantling this asset. Because the asset was already retired in a previous, now closed, month, you can no longer post this invoice to the asset. Instead, you let Accounts Payable handle the transaction just as it would all other invoices.

Nevertheless, you would like to show this transaction on the Asset Retirements report because you consider the dismantling cost part of the asset scrap, which, in turn, has an impact on the amount of loss shown on the report. Therefore, SAP's Asset Accounting allows you to post subsequent costs to this asset using transaction type 285 (or transaction type 286 for subsequent revenue postings).

This posting is just a statistical posting however, meaning that it is posted to the sub-ledger only and not posted to the General Ledger. The Asset Retirements report will show this statistical amount in a separate column (see Figure 3.7).

As you can see in Figure 3.7, the report includes a field for subsequent costs (**Ret. costs**) and a field for subsequent revenue (**Ret. revenue**). The example for subsequent revenue would be that you receive sales proceeds for an asset that you had scrapped earlier.

Asset	SNo.	Cap.date	Asset description		Retirement	Depr. retired	Ret. book value	Crcy
		Deact.Date	Asset description		Ret. revenue	Loss	Gain	
					Ret. costs			
	DocumentNo	Pstng Date	Text		"	"	"	Crcy
		Ast.val.dt	TType Reference	Quantity BUn	"	"	"	
5001	0	08/23/1996	Finish Sander		37,850.00-	0.00	37,850.00-	USD
		01/01/1997			0.00	37,850.00-	0.00	
					0.00			
	100000092	01/01/1997			37,850.00-	0.00	37,850.00-	USD
		01/01/1997	200		0.00	37,850.00-	0.00	
					0.00			

Figure 3.6 Asset Retirements Report – Detailed Version

Asset	SNo.	Cap.date	Asset description		Retirement	Depr. retired	Ret. book value	Crcy
		Deact.Date	Asset description		Ret. revenue	Loss	Gain	
					Ret. costs			
	DocumentNo	Pstng Date	Text		"	"	"	Crcy
		Ast.val.dt	TType Reference	Quantity BUn	"	"	"	
3405	0	03/25/2006	SEEMA CHAIRS		10,000.00-	1,667.00	8,333.00-	EUR
		10/31/2006			0.00	9,333.00-	0.00	
					1,000.00			
		11/30/2006			0.00	0.00	0.00	EUR
		10/31/2006	285		0.00	1,000.00-	0.00	
					1,000.00			
	100000777	11/25/2006			10,000.00-	1,667.00	8,333.00-	EUR
		10/31/2006	250		0.00	8,333.00-	0.00	
					0.00			

Figure 3.7 Asset Retirements Report with Statistical Retirement Costs

3.4 Asset Transfers Report

Asset transfers are a normal business event and can include intra-company transfers (transfers between assets within the same company code) and inter-company transfers (transfers between two company codes). The *Asset Transfers* report includes intra-company transfers only and shows the cost amount transferred and the corresponding depreciation adjustments.

The information required to access the Asset Transfers report is as follows:

▶ **Menu Path**
Accounting • Financial Accounting • Fixed Assets • Information System • Reports on Asset Accounting • Day-to-Day Activities • International • Intracompany Asset Transfers
▶ **Transaction Code**
S_ALR_87012054
▶ **Technical Report Name**
RAUMBU_ALV01

Main Report Purpose and Recipients

This report shows asset transfers (transfers from one asset to another asset). It includes the amount of cost and depreciation transferred. The main recipients for the report are general asset accounting departments.

The Selection Screen

The selection screen for the Asset Transfers report, again, is identical to the other transaction-based reports.

Report Output

Just like the other transaction reports, the Asset Transfers report includes detailed information for each transfer, such as document number, posting date, transaction type, etc. For the default Asset Transfers report output, see Figure 3.8.

Specifying Transaction Types

One thing to remember is that SAP considers settlements from an AuC to a final fixed asset a transfer (i.e., a transfer from one asset to another, to be exact). The default transaction types involved are 33x and 34x.

As was already mentioned, you may want to report these types of *transfers* as acquisitions in the Asset Acquisitions report. After all, in the US, we would consider these settlement transactions the in-service placement for the final asset.

The Asset Transfers report works just like the other transaction reports. If you leave the **Transaction type** selection field blank, the report will use SAP's default logic to determine whether a transaction can be considered a transfer. If, however, you enter specific transaction types in the selection screen, the report will show only these transactions on the report output (in other words, it's a transaction type override feature).

Caveat

One drawback of the Asset Transfers report is that it does not show where an asset was transferred to or from. It seems like a very basic reporting requirement of any transfer report, but for one reason or another this information not is not included.

Therefore, I usually advise my clients to create a custom transfer report using tools such as SQVI (SAP Quick Viewer). Figure 3.9 shows a simple example of an such an enhanced Asset Transfers report. Notice that it includes a separate column showing the transfer **To/from Asset**. To me, having visibility of the complete transfer (including transfer-from and transfer-to asset numbers) is critical to a meaningful transfer report.

Creating such an enhanced Asset Transfers report is a simple task. It took me just a few minutes to create the example shown in Figure 3.9 using standard SQVI functionality.

```
 Asset      SNo. Cap.date  Asset description                                  Transfer      TransODep      TransSDep Crcy
         DocumentNo Pstng Date TType Ast.val.dt Reference        Quantity BUn  Transfer      TransODep      TransSDep Crcy
                    Text

 1104        0    01/01/1993 Production Building, Los Angeles Plant          1,062,961.00-  263,780.00       0.00 USD
          100000007 01/01/1997 300   01/01/1997                              1,062,961.00-  263,780.00       0.00 USD
```

Figure 3.8 Default Asset Transfer Report Layout

Fixed Asset Transfer Report

Choose Save

Fixed Asset Transfer Report

CoCd	Asset	SNo.	DocumentNo	AsstVal date	TTy	To/from Asset		Σ Amount posted	Crcy	Σ Ord.dep.on trans
MMC1	20005	0	14	05/04/2006	320	30000	0	12,000.00-	USD	1,142.86
MMC1	30001	0	16	05/04/2006	320	20006	0	10,000.00-	USD	666.67
MMC1	30002	0	16	05/04/2006	320	20007	0	15,000.00-	USD	1,000.00
							▪	**37,000.00-**	**USD** ▪	**2,809.53**

Figure 3.9 Enhanced Asset Transfer Report

3.5 Asset Transactions Report

The reports we've looked at so far (i.e., the Asset Acquisitions, Asset Retirements, and Asset Transfer reports) apply an internal filter criteria to determine what is considered to be an acquisition posting, retirement, or transfer. This filter uses settings from the transaction type group to determine what a transaction should be classified as. This might work well in most instances but, as explained earlier when discussing the acquisition reports, the reports may not always adhere to the accounting principle you would like to apply. Therefore, the standard acquisition report with its default transaction type filter might not be a good report for you to use, depending on your asset capitalization process.

The good news is that the solution to this problem is quite simple. All you have to do is limit the report to a specific range of transaction types that you consider to be acquisitions, according to your accounting rules. Following this approach makes the **Asset Transactions** report very powerful, because you could use it to report any asset posting in any way you want to, simply by limiting the report to specific transaction types.

The information required to access the Asset Transactions report is as follows:

- **Menu Path**
  Accounting • Financial Accounting • Fixed Assets • Information System • Reports on Asset Accounting • Day-to-Day Activities • International • Asset transactions
- **Transaction Code**
  S_ALR_87012048
- **Technical Report Name**
  RABEWG_ALV01

Main Report Purpose and Recipients

This is a powerful report that can be used to report any asset transaction (be it acquisitions, retirements, transfers, etc.) according to your specifications. Main recipients of this report are general asset accounting departments and tax departments.

Creating a Custom Report Variant

For example, a common scenario is the issue of charitable donations. From an accounting perspective, a charitable donation of an asset is nothing but an asset retirement without revenue (also known as an asset scrap). For tax purposes, however, you must be able to report these donation transactions separately from the normal retirement transactions. All you would have to do is run this Asset Transactions report and limit it to the transaction types you use for the charitable donations. This will show only these donations and not any of the normal asset retirements.

Once you create a custom report, you could save it as a variant so that you don't have to enter the selection criteria every time you want to run this report. Figure 3.10 shows the Asset Transactions report for a charitable donations scenario. As you can see, it shows the transac-

```
Asset       SNo. Cap.date   Asset description                    Retirement   Depr. retired  Ret. book value
                 Deact.Date Asset description                   Ret. revenue           Loss             Gain
                                                                  Ret. costs
      DocumentNo Pstng Date Text                                           "              "                "
                 Ast.val.dt TType Reference         Quantity BUn             "              "
                                                                           "

3324           0 05/03/1999 PC Techn. Service PB7663               1,302.77-      1,302.77             0.00
                 01/01/2007                                            0.00           0.00             0.00
                                                                       0.00
       100000017 04/01/2007                                         1,302.77-      1,302.77             0.00
                 01/01/2007 Z20                                          0.00           0.00             0.00
                                                                       0.00
```

Figure 3.10 Asset Transactions Report Limited to Specific Transaction Type

tion type **Z20** which was set up as a Charitable Donations transaction.

You could now click the **Save** icon on the selection screen and save this report as a variant. To make things easy, you can enter a **Meaning** for this variant (i.e. **Charitable Donations Report**) as shown in Figure 3.11.

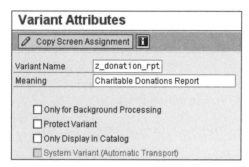

Figure 3.11 Save Report as a Variant

The next time you start the Asset Transactions report, you can simply click the **Get Variants** icon and then select the **Charitable Donations Report** variant (see Figure 3.12). It will then automatically fill in the corresponding selection screen fields, including the transaction type limitation.

Variant catalog for program RABEWG_ALV01	
Variant name	Short description
SAP&001	SAP Standard Variant
SAP&AUDIT_110	Other Capitlzd In-House Prod.
SAP&AUDIT_ZUSH	Audit
SAP&HERKUNFT	Proof of Origin
Z_DONATION_RP	Charitable Donations Report

Figure 3.12 Select Variant

Using different variants for this Asset Transactions report allows you to create a re-usable library of asset reports that anyone can use without having to re-enter the transaction type limitations.

3.6 List of Origins by Asset Debits Report

The *List of Origins by Asset Debits* report is a powerful report you can use to analyze the origin of an asset's value. In other words, it shows where the acquisition amounts (debits) came from. The report shows the asset's acquisition cost and the information related to the source of these amounts (i.e., the document number, total amount vs. settled amount, cost element, etc.).

The information required to access the List of Origins by Asset Debits report is as follows:

> ▶ **Menu Path**
> Accounting • Financial Accounting • Fixed Assets • Information System • Reports on Asset Accounting • Day-to-Day Activities • International • List of Origins by Asset Debits
> ▶ **Transaction Code**
> S_ALR_87012058
> ▶ **Technical Report Name**
> RAHERK01

Main Report Purpose and Recipients
This report is intended to help you analyze where the costs for an asset came from (i.e., the project or WBS element number, vendor number, cost element, etc.). The main recipients of this report are general asset accounting and financial accounting departments.

The Selection Screen
The List of Origins by Asset Debits report uses a modified version of the basic selection screen. Under **Further settings**, you will find two options, as shown in Figure 3.13:
▶ **Display reversal transactions**
When you select this option, the report will include reversal transactions (which ultimately don't affect the asset's cost, because the settlement amounts went in and out of the asset account).
▶ **Display orig. line itms**
This option is useful for settlements from investment measures or AuCs. When selected, the report will include detailed information regarding the postings made to the individual asset (i.e., the original amounts versus the settled amounts, individual document numbers, etc.).

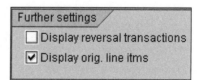

Figure 3.13 Display Reversal Transactions and Display Original Line Items

Report Output

When the option **Display orig. line itms** is not selected, the report output includes the asset's cost and the document numbers that make up the cost, as shown in Figure 3.14.

Notice in Figure 3.14 that asset **900011386** has a cost of $2,826.85. This amount was posted on **04/30/2007** with document number **100000420**. The report even includes the WBS element number from where this posting originated.

Now let's look at the same asset, but this time we'll select the option **Display orig. line itms** on the selection screen. Figure 3.15 shows how the report output has changed.

> **Note**
>
> You can use the **Display orig. line itms** option only for depreciation area 01.

As you can see in Figure 3.15, the report now displays two additional line items for asset **900011386**. It shows the original invoices that were posted to the WBS ele-

ment in 2006 (document numbers **1100013853** and **1100013822**). Also, it shows the total invoice amount (**$16,190.52** and **$16,190.40** respectively) and how much of these amounts was actually settled to this particular asset (**$1,413.43** and **$1,413.42**). To the right of this information, the report shows the vendor number of the vendor who submitted the invoice and the cost element used to post the invoices.

This report provides a very powerful reporting feature, because it can show you all invoices and transactions that were used to post an asset's acquisition cost.

3.7 List of Origins by Cost Element Report

The *List of Origins by Cost Element* report is very similar to the List of Origins by Asset Debits report. But instead of showing the individual line items used to post an asset's acquisition cost, this report shows the individual cost elements used to post to the asset. In other words, this report shows the asset's acquisition cost separated by cost element.

Main number SNo. DocumentNo FY	Capit.date Name PostngDate TTy AstValDate Text	Acquis; Partial acquis;	Origin
900011386 0	04/30/2007 Microcomputador DELL gx 620+teclado	2,826.85	
100000420 2007	04/30/2007 331 04/30/2007 WBS C2BZA060342006CD	2,826.85	Inv.WBS el C2BZA060342006CD05
900011387 0	04/30/2007 Microcomputador DELL gx 620+teclado	2,826.85	
100000420 2007	04/30/2007 331 04/30/2007 WBS C2BZA060342006CD	2,826.85	Inv.WBS el C2BZA060342006CD05
Assetclass	228 Computers - PC's *	5,653.70	

Figure 3.14 List of Origins without Original Line Item Display

Main number SNo. DocumentNo FY	Capit.date Name PostngDate TTy AstValDate Text Orig. amount ;	Acquis; Partial acquis; Settlmt.amount	Origin Original origin	Cost elem.
900011386 0	04/30/2007 Microcomputador DELL gx 620+teclado	2,826.85		
100000420 2007	04/30/2007 331 04/30/2007 WBS C2BZA060342006CD	2,826.85	Inv.WBS el C2BZA060342006CD05	
1100013853 2006	16,190.52 =	1,413.43	Vendor 0004503937	4300007
1100013822 2006	16,190.40 +	1,413.42	Vendor 0004503937	4300007
900011387 0	04/30/2007 Microcomputador DELL gx 620+teclado	2,826.85		
100000420 2007	04/30/2007 331 04/30/2007 WBS C2BZA060342006CD	2,826.85	Inv.WBS el C2BZA060342006CD05	
1100013853 2006	16,190.52 =	1,413.43	Vendor 0004503937	4300007
1100013822 2006	16,190.40 +	1,413.42	Vendor 0004503937	4300007
Assetclass	228 Computers - PC's *	5,653.70		

Figure 3.15 List of Origins with Original Line Item Display

The information required to access the List of Origins by Cost Element report is as follows:

> ▶ **Menu Path**
> **Accounting • Financial Accounting • Fixed Assets • Information System • Reports on Asset Accounting • Day-to-Day Activities • International • List of Origins by Cost Element**
> ▶ **Transaction Code**
> **S_ALR_87012060**
> ▶ **Technical Report Name**
> **RAHERK02**

Main Report Purpose and Recipients

This report is intended to help you analyze how the cost for an asset has been posted by separate cost element (i.e., material versus labor versus overhead charges, etc.). The main recipients of this report are general asset accounting and financial accounting departments.

The Selection Screen

The List of Origins by Cost Element report uses a version of the basic selection screen, but there are two noteworthy changes. First, the selection screen doesn't have a report date field or a depreciation area field. It doesn't need these two selection fields because all values shown are from depreciation area 01, as of the current date. Secondly, the selection screen includes an option called **Display information on origin**, as shown in Figure 3.16. When you select this option, the report includes information for the original postings made to this asset, such as cost center, plant, or material.

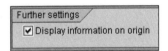

Figure 3.16 Display Information on Origin Option

Report Output

Figure 3.17 shows the default report output, which includes the asset's acquisition cost and a list of cost elements used to post this acquisition amount. Furthermore, this list includes the fiscal year when the costs were incurred, as well as information on the investment measure (i.e., WBS element or internal order number) to which the costs were posted.

Notice in Figure 3.17 that asset **900010771** has a cost of **$26,075.44**. This amount was posted with the four cost elements shown just below the asset. For example, the report shows that **$2,173.58** in professional service fees was included in the asset's cost. Other cost elements commonly used for tracking asset cost include material charges, labor (in-house or contract), overhead charges, etc.

This report provides a useful reporting feature to show the acquisition cost for an asset by cost elements, provided that different cost elements have been used when the original charges were recorded.

3.8 Chapter Summary

This chapter introduced you to the most commonly used transaction-based reports in Asset Accounting. After reading this chapter, you should have a good understanding of the main reports used to show asset transactions. The reports to remember from this chapter are:

▶ **Asset Acquisitions**
This report lists all asset acquisition transactions, including detailed information such as document number, posting date, and transaction types. Make sure to include/exclude the correct transaction types that are considered asset acquisitions according to your specific accounting rules.

Main number SNo.	Capit.date Description	Acq.value	Origin object	Text
FY	Cost elem. Text	Portion of APC	Plnt Material number	Material short text
	Cost ctr. ActTyp Text	Portion of APC		
900010771　0	04/28/2006 4 Postos de Trabalho	26,075.44		
2005 4100028	Profess. Svcs	2,173.58-	WBS C2BZA050192005CD05	Machinery and Equipm
2005 4300007	Machinery & Equip	27,169.18	WBS C2BZA050192005CD05	Machinery and Equipm
2005 5900019	Other S&S - Aviation	769.76	WBS C2BZA050192005CD05	Machinery and Equipm
2006 4300007	Machinery & Equip	310.08	WBS C2BZA050192005CD05	Machinery and Equipm

Figure 3.17 List of Origins by Cost Element

► **Asset Retirements**

This report shows all asset retirements (with and without revenue) and includes information such as the resulting gain and loss amount, sales proceeds, and statistical subsequent cost and revenue.

► **Asset Transfers (intra-company)**

This report includes intra-company transfers only (inter-company transfers are reported via the acquisition and Retirements reports). In other words, it includes the transfer cost and depreciation amounts but unfortunately, does not include the transfer-to asset number.

► **Asset Transactions**

This report can be used to report any asset transaction in any way you want, by simply entering the specific transaction types on the selection screen. Once you limit the Asset Transactions report to the desired transaction type, you can save it as a variant and create a library of custom asset reports that can be reused at any time without having to re-enter the selection limitations.

► **List of Origins by Asset Debits**

This report shows the individual debits or line items used to post an asset's acquisition cost and includes information such as the original document numbers, vendor accounts, and settlement amounts. This report is most useful when the option Display orig. line itms is selected.

► **List of Origins by Cost Elements**

This report is very similar to the List of Origins by Asset Debits report, however, instead of showing the asset's cost by individual line items, this report shows the cost by different cost elements.

In Chapter 4, you'll learn about the most important asset report of them all – the *Asset History Sheet* report. This is by far the most important report to know in Asset Accounting, because it combines the best of balance-based and transaction-based reports and can be configured to meet your specific reporting requirements. No other report offers this for Asset Accounting.

4 Asset History Sheet Report

Now that you know about several important balance-based and transaction-based reports in Asset Accounting, you'll learn about the most important and most powerful report – the *Asset History Sheet* report. It is a very unique report, because it combines balance-based reporting with transactional reporting in one report.

The basic Asset History Sheet report features a roll-forward layout starting with the beginning asset balances, followed by asset activity (transactions), and then the ending balances. All amount columns and the entire report layout can be customized to fit your specific reporting requirements. In other words, the report can show any transaction in any way you deem correct.

For example, just because SAP considers a transaction an acquisition, you don't have to show this transaction as an acquisition (you might consider it a special type of acquisition (a merger acquisition, for example) and therefore, want to display it separately from the regular acquisition postings on this report.

Unlike most of the other asset reports that are ready to use in the standard SAP system, the Asset History Sheet report requires the configuration of a specific Asset History Sheet version and various other settings. We'll discuss the required configuration in detail in Section 4.2, but first, let's look at the report more closely.

4.1 Asset History Sheet Report

The *Asset History Sheet* report is by far the most powerful report at your disposal, yet it is also the most commonly underutilized report. The reason for this may be that the report is so complex that it might seem overwhelming at times.

The information required to access the Asset History Sheet report is as follows:

▶ **Menu Path**
Accounting • Financial Accounting • Fixed Assets • Information System • Reports on Asset Accounting • Notes to Financial Statements • International • Asset History Sheet

▶ **Transaction Code**
S_ALR_87011990

▶ **Technical Report Name**
RAGITT_ALV01

Main Report Purpose and Recipients

This report is the most comprehensive asset report in roll-forward layout (beginning balances, asset activity, ending balances). The report can be completely customized to meet your reporting requirements and should be the basis for all asset reporting and reconciliation. The main recipients of this report are general accounting and tax departments.

The Selection Screen

Before we look at the actual report output, let's examine the selection screen of the report. The selection screen is very similar to the one used for the Total Depreciation report. One additional and critical difference, however, is the field for the **History sheet version** shown in Figure 4.1.

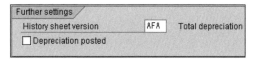

Figure 4.1 Specifiy History Sheet Version

Specifying the History sheet version is required to run this report. It controls the entire report layout because it

Asset	SNo.	Asset description	Σ	APC FY start	Σ	Dep. FY start	Σ	Bk.val.FY strt	Σ	Acquisition	Σ	Dep. for year	Σ	Retirement	Σ	Dep.retir.	Σ	Trans
1105	0	Distribution center Seattle		850,369.00		67,024.00-		783,345.00		0.00		17,008.00-		0.00		0.00		0.
1106	0	Administration Building, Los Angeles		31,888,830.00		2,513,331.00-		29,375,499.00		0.00		637,777.00-		0.00		0.00		0.
1107	0	Sales Office South		773,250.00		32,219.00-		741,031.00		0.00		15,465.00-		0.00		0.00		0.
1108	0	Plant I - Warehouse Central Street		484,570.00		29,076.00-		455,494.00		0.00		0.00		0.00		0.00		484,570.

Figure 4.2 Basic Asset History Sheet Report Layout

specifies how many columns and rows the report will display. Also, and even more importantly, it determines what transactions are included in this report and how these transactions are being reported. In other words, the history sheet version acts almost like your very own report writer. You can customize every detail of this report in the corresponding configuration transactions and that's what makes this report so powerful.

Report Output

Let's take a look at Figure 4.2, which shows a sample output of the report. The report is very wide and can include up to eight value columns (plus asset main number and subnumber, description, capitalization date, etc.); therefore, we'll look at only the first few columns here. However, we'll look at all of the columns at some point in this section.

Note

The Basic Asset History Sheet report features a basic *roll-forward* layout – in other words, the amounts shown roll forward, or add up, as you go from left to right. Also note that the report shown in Figure 4.2 uses history sheet version 0001.

Beginning and Ending Balances

You can see in Figure 4.3 that the report shows the beginning balances (acquisition cost, accumulated depreciation, and net book value) for each asset. These values are always as of the beginning of the reporting year.

Σ	APC FY start	Σ	Dep. FY start	Σ	Bk.val.FY strt
	850,369.00		67,024.00-		783,345.00
	31,888,830.00		2,513,331.00-		29,375,499.00
	773,250.00		32,219.00-		741,031.00

Figure 4.3 Beginning Values

When you scroll to the very right of the report, as shown in Figure 4.4, you will find the columns for the ending bal-

ances (again, cost, depreciation, net book value) as of the reporting date that you entered on the selection screen.

Σ	Current APC	Σ	Accumul. dep.	Σ	Curr.bk.val.
	850,369.00		84,032.00-		766,337.00
	31,888,830.00		3,151,108.00-		28,737,722.00
	773,250.00		47,684.00-		725,566.00

Figure 4.4 Ending Values

Cross-checking Amounts

The beginning and ending balance columns correspond to the balance-based reports we discussed in Chapter 2 and therefore you should be able to cross-check amounts. Specifically, you should be able to use the Asset Balances report (see Section 2.1 for details) or the Total Depreciation report (see Section 2.3) to compare the amounts. If you used the same selection criteria, the amounts should match.

Asset Activities

Let's now get back to the Asset History Sheet report. In between the beginning and ending balance columns, the report shows the various asset activities (acquisition postings, retirements, transfers, etc.) (see Figure 4.5). Again, the way the report shows these amounts is completely configurable according to your specific reporting requirements.

These activity columns should correspond directly to the individual Asset Transaction reports we discussed in Chapter 3. For example, the **Retirements** column in the Asset History Sheet report should equal the retirement amount reported on the Asset Retirements report (see Section 3.3). Consequently, you can use the Asset History Sheet report to reconcile all other transaction-based reports.

Standard Asset History Sheet Caveats

The examples you've seen so far have used Asset History Sheet version 0001. This is an SAP-supplied example that

≡ Acquisition	≡	Dep. for year	≡ Retirement	≡ Dep.retir.	≡	Transfer	≡ Dep.transfer	≡ Post-capital.	≡ Dep.post-cap.	≡ Invest.support	≡ Write-ups
37,500.00		3,750.00-	0.00	0.00		0.00	0.00	0.00	0.00	0.00	0.00
0.00		3,600.00-	0.00	0.00		36,000.00	7,650.00-	0.00	0.00	0.00	0.00
0.00		4,100.00-	0.00	0.00		41,000.00	8,713.00-	0.00	0.00	0.00	0.00

Figure 4.5 Asset Activity

```
Report date 12/31/1997    Asset History Sheet - 01 Book deprec.
 Created on 04/01/2007    In compl. w/EC directive 4 (13 col.,wide version) (incomplete)
```

Figure 4.6 Asset History Sheet Report Header

comes with every standard SAP system (among several other versions). However, these are only examples and not necessarily intended for you to use in a live production SAP system, especially if you're running a report for the US.

One of the main reasons is that the acquisitions shown in the SAP example follow the accounting logic described in Chapter 3 for the standard SAP acquisition report (that is, the report considers settlements from AuC to final assets transfers rather than acquisitions, which is what we need in the US). Therefore, the version used in this example would not be appropriate for any reliable reporting for the US.

For example, take a look at Figure 4.6, which shows the header of the report. Notice that the header says **In compl. w/ EC directive 4**, which stands for *In compliance with European Community directive 4*. In other words, this particular Asset History Sheet version is according to European GAAP accounting rules!

Also, the header includes the word **incomplete**, which indicates that this particular Asset History Sheet version does not include all transactions and values that may

have been posted to assets. What this means is that there may be values missing from this report!

This is one more reason why you really need to create your own customized Asset History Sheet version. It's the only way to guarantee that you capture all asset transactions in this report, as well as show these transactions in a manner consistent with your location's specific accounting rules.

A Sample Custom Asset History Sheet

In my work as a consultant, I have created hundreds of different Asset History Sheet versions for my clients. While you are, of course, free to create any layout that meets your company's requirements, I've noticed that my clients have used one particular layout more often than other layouts. Figure 4.7 shows what this sample layout looks like.

This particular layout is a copy of the standard delivered Asset History Sheet version 0001; however, it includes the following extra fields and variations:

	A	B	C	D	E	F	G	H
1					**Asset History Sheet Version**			
2	FY Beginning APC	CIP IN	Acquisitions	Retirements	Interco. Transfers IN	Intraco. Transfers IN	Other Adjustments	FY Ending APC
3	FY Beginning DDA	CIP OUT	Depreciation	Dep. Retirements	Dep. Interco. Trsf. IN	Dep. Intraco. Trsf. IN	Dep. Other Adjustm.	FY Ending DDA
4	FY Beginning NBV				Interco. Transfers OUT	Intraco. Transfers OUT		FY Ending NBV
5					Dep. Interco. Trsf. OUT	Dep. Intraco. Trsf. OUT		
6								
7								
8	APC	Acquisition and Production Cost						
9	DDA	Depreciation, Depletion & Amortization						
10	NBV	Net Book Value						
11								
12								
13	CIP IN	Lists all incoming CIP transactions (monthly settlements from orders/WBS)						
14	CIP OUT	List all outgoing CIP transactions (final settlements from order/WBS)						
15								
16	Other Adjustments	List all other asset transactions, such as post-capitalizations, write-ups, tax audit adjustments, etc.						

Figure 4.7 Asset History Sheet Version Template

▶ **CIP (Construction In Progress) In and CIP Out**
These two fields show the movements in and out of the CIP account (i.e., the debits and credits to AuC). The benefit of having a CIP In/Out column is that it can show the net activity for assets-placed-in-service in two separate fields.

▶ **Intra- and Inter-company Transfers In and Out**
If your company posts asset transfers (either within the same company code or between company codes), you might be interested in displaying the transfers-in separately from the transfers-out, and creating these columns allows you to do just that.

▶ **Other Adjustments**
Most of my clients would agree with the following statement: If a transaction is not an acquisition, retirement, or transfer, it must be an *other adjustment*. These transactions typically include rarely posted transactions such as impairments, revaluations, post-capitalizations, tax audit adjustments, and the like. It wouldn't make much sense to create separate columns for each of these transactions. A better idea, I think, would be to group together all of these transactions in a column called **Other Adjustments**.

Now, if you have a specific reporting requirement and would like to show the impairments in a separate column, simply create one or even create a new separate Asset History Sheet version. You can create as many versions as necessary (i.e., you may have a special version for book purposes and a separate one for tax purposes).

Figure 4.8 shows what a final custom layout similar to this one can look like in Asset Accounting. The final layout depends on your particular business needs (i.e., do you even post intercompany transfers, etc.). I created this version for one of my clients who didn't have any specific requirements for intercompany transfers (i.e., they only have one company code); therefore, I didn't create a separate column for these kinds of transfers.

Most importantly, notice the report header in Figure 4.8. The description **Asset History Sheet/Roll-forward Report (complete)** indicates that this is a custom Asset History Sheet version and that the report is complete. These are two very important indicators that you should always pay attention to when working with the Asset History Sheet report.

Reconciling the Asset History Sheet Report

At the end of the year, it's a good idea to reconcile the Asset History Sheet report with all of the individual Asset Transaction reports and the Asset Balances report or Total Depreciation report. This validates all beginning balances, asset activity throughout the year, and ending balances using various reports (independent from each other). Once you have reconciled the asset values within the Asset Accounting module, you should then reconcile the ending balances to the individual G/L account balances (i.e., via Transaction **FS10N** – Account Balance display). When all numbers reconcile, you can happily forward these reports to the auditors!

| Report date 12/31/2004 | Asset History Sheet – 01 Book deprec. | | | | | |
| Created on 08/14/2004 | Asset History Sheet/Roll-forward Report (complete) | | | | | |

CompanyCode

Asset	SNo.	Cap.date	Asset description		Crcy		
APC FY start		AuC In	Acquisition	Retirement	Transfer	Oth.Adjustm.	Current APC
Dep. FY start		AuC Out	Dep. for year	Dep.retir.	Dep.transfer	Dep.Oth.Adj.	Accumul. dep.
Bk.val.FY strt							Curr.bk.val.
4006175	0	03/31/2004	SEMI-AUTOMATIC BAGGER		USD		
0.00		0.00	13,160.80	0.00	0.00	0.00	13,160.80
0.00		0.00	1,096.74-	0.00	0.00	0.00	1,096.74-
0.00							12,064.06
6001013	0	12/31/2003	CBRN Tooling Continued		USD		
344,380.39		169,303.51	0.00	0.00	0.00	0.00	0.00
0.00		513,683.90-	0.00	0.00	0.00	0.00	0.00
344,380.39							0.00

Figure 4.8 Example for a Custom Asset History Sheet Version

4.2 Configuration

At first glance, the configuration required for the Asset History Sheet report may seem overwhelmingly complex, but don't despair. We'll break it into manageable tasks and you'll see that it all comes down to assigning one object to another object.

Transaction Types

First, remember that all fixed asset transactions must be posted with a transaction type. In Asset Accounting, the transaction type is assigned to an Asset History Sheet group. See the **Asst hist sheet grp** field in the **Other features** section shown in Figure 4.9.

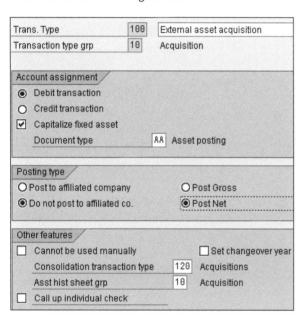

Figure 4.9 Transaction Type Configuration

The Asset History Sheet group is nothing more than a numerical key and a description. Its only purpose is to group together similar transaction types. For example, the SAP system delivers several retirement transaction types (i.e., transaction type 200 – asset scrap, transaction type 201 – asset retirement due to force majeur, transaction type 210 – asset sale, etc.). All of these transaction types are similar in nature, because they ultimately post a retirement transaction to an asset. Therefore, you could assign all these similar transaction types to the same Asset History Sheet group.

SAP-Delivered Asset History Sheet Groups

In the standard system, SAP already delivers approximately 25 Asset History Sheet groups (see Figure 4.10 for a list).

Grp	Name asset hist. sheet group
10	Acquisition
12	Reverse acquisition in following years
15	Down payment
20	Retirement
25	Retirement of curr-yr acquisition
30	Retirmt transfer of prior-yr acquis.
31	Acquiring transfer of prior-yr acquis.
32	Retirmt transfer of curr-yr acquis.
33	Acquiring transfer of curr-yr acquis.
34	Retirmt transfer of prior-yr acquis. from AuC
35	Acquiring transfer of prior-yr acquis. from AuC
36	Retirmt transfer of curr-yr acquis. from AuC
37	Acquiring transfer of curr-yr acquis. from AuC
40	Post-capitalization
50	Allocation of investment support
70	Write-up special and ord. depreciation
71	Write-up ordinary depreciation
72	Write-up special tax depreciation
73	Write-up unplanned depreciation
74	Write-up reserve transfer
75	Write-up all deprec. types
YA	Accum.values as of FY start (History sheet)
YY	Annual values (History sheet)
YZ	Accum.values as of FY end (History sheet)

Figure 4.10 Standard SAP History Sheet Groups

Creating Custom Asset History Sheet Groups

Of course, you're free to set up your own Asset History Sheet groups according to your own requirements using configuration Transaction **OAV9**. SAP also makes default assignments of most transaction types to Asset History Sheet groups. For example, transaction type 200 and 201 are both assigned to Asset History Sheet group 20 (Retirements). In most cases, the SAP assignment should be in accordance to your reporting requirements, but we know that there are special circumstances where you would want to show a transaction differently than SAP's default. Let's look at an example.

Remember the issue we discussed in Section 3.2 with the acquisition postings? Transaction type 331 is used to post prior-year spending from an AuC to a final asset in the current year. By default, SAP considers this transaction a transfer and not an acquisition. While this is in compliance with European accounting rules, it is not what we want in the US. This transaction type is by default assigned to Asset History Sheet group 35 (**Acquiring transfer prior-yr acquis.**) as shown in Figure 4.11.

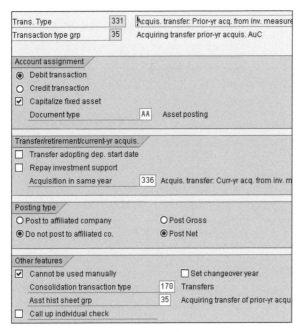

Figure 4.11 Transaction Type 331 Configuration

Depending on your situation, you may want to consider reassigning this transaction type to a different group, such as an acquisitions group, to better suit your needs.

Reassignment Considerations

You must, however, always consider the impact that a reassignment could have on other businesses in your system, which use the same key. For example, if you have a German company code and a US company code in the same SAP system and both are using the same transaction type, a re-assignment would cause problems for the German company because they would still want to show this transaction as a transfer.

So, what's the answer? Can only one reporting requirement be satisfied? The answer, of course, is no. SAP's Asset Accounting is a very flexible system and can accommodate multiple reporting requirements at the same time. The answer to the aforementioned problem is to create multiple Asset History Sheet versions and custom Asset History Sheet groups to address the individual reporting requirements. This takes us to the next configuration task

for the Asset History Sheet, namely, assigning Asset History Sheet groups to the Asset History Sheet version.

Assigning Asset History Sheet Groups to Asset History Sheet Version Positions

Once you have assigned all transaction types to the desired Asset History Sheet groups, you need to assign these groups to the Asset History Sheet version, or, more specifically, to a position within the version. The version defines the layout of the entire Asset History Sheet report. See Figure 4.12, which shows a sample version via Transaction **OA79**.

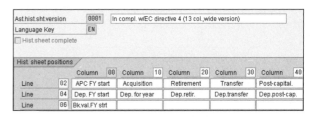

Figure 4.12 Sample Asset History Sheet Layout

Notice, for example, the field (or position) labeled **Acquisition**. When you double-click this position, you get into the detailed screen shown in Figure 4.13. On the left, you see all Asset History Sheet groups, and to the right, you see several columns. The columns correspond to the posting amounts for the asset cost and depreciation (separated by depreciation type: ordinary, special, unplanned, etc.). Each cell in these columns contains either an *X* or a period (.), or it's blank.

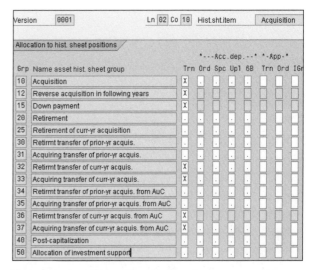

Figure 4.13 Asset History Sheet Configuration

An *X* in a column means that you want to show the particular value from that column and Asset History Sheet group in the position that you are currently in. A period means that this cell has already been assigned somewhere else in the Asset History Sheet version, while a blank space means that this cell has not been assigned yet. Confused? Let's walk through an example together.

Note

Make sure to double-check all assignments across all cells. You can assign cells twice without receiving any warning message from the SAP system, and consequently run the risk of accidentally doubling values in your report.

An Assignment Example

Let's take a simple asset retirement transaction – transaction type 200. The configuration screen (Transaction **AO74**) shows you that the transaction type is assigned to Asset History Sheet group 20 (Retirement) – see the **Asst hist sheet grp** field in the **Other features** section in Figure 4.14.

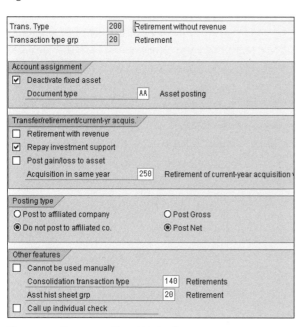

Figure 4.14 Transaction Type 200 Configuration

Now let's look at a sample Asset History Sheet version in configuration (Transaction **OA79**), using version 0001 (see Figure 4.12 again). Here, the third column contains

the two fields (also called positions) **Retirement** and **Dep. retir.** The first field is supposed to show the retired cost amount for an asset, while the second field is supposed to show the associated depreciation amount for the same retirement posting. Double-click the position **Retirement** and you should see the screen shown in Figure 4.15.

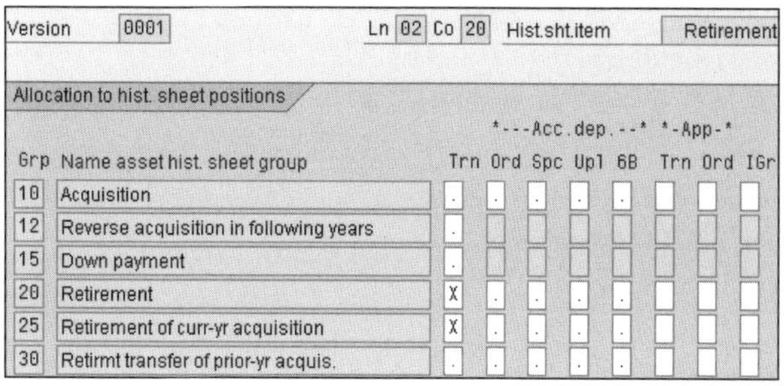

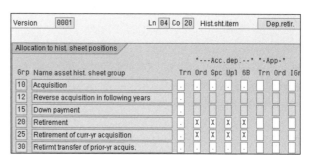

Figure 4.15 Retirement Position

Notice that Asset History Sheet group **20** (Retirement) has an **X** in the value column labeled **Trn** (for Transactional Amount). This makes the retirement amount from the asset posting show up in this particular position (but just the retired cost amount, not the depreciation).

Now go to the previous screen and double-click the position labeled **Dep.retir.** The screen shown in Figure 4.16 appears.

Figure 4.16 Depreciation for Retirement Position

For Asset History Sheet group **20**, you now see that the **Trn** column contains a period (.) This indicates that this value has already been assigned in this version. The following four columns contain an **X**. These columns correspond to the depreciation amounts of the retirement posting (separated by depreciation type: ordinary, special, unplanned, and 6B depreciation). Due to this assignment, the depreciation adjustment amounts of the retirement posting will show up in this position.

> **Note**
> 6B depreciation refers to a special German type of depreciation also known as Transfer of Reserves.

Finally, you'll notice that the last three columns are left blank and are not assigned. They represent transactional values and depreciation amounts for Revaluation transactions, which are not applicable to this retirement scenario.

A Summary of the Example

Let's summarize this example. Retirement transaction type 200 is assigned to Asset History Sheet group 20 (retirement). The Asset History Sheet version (that's the layout of my specific Asset History Sheet report) contains two positions to show the asset's retirement cost amount and the associated depreciation adjustment. Each position has its own column position in the configuration Transaction **OA79**. The asset's cost amount is represented by the column labeled **Trn** (for transactional amount), while the depreciation amounts are represented by the columns labeled **Ord** (ordinary depreciation), **Spc** (special depreciation), **Upl** (unplanned depreciation), and **6B** (transfer of reserves).

This assignment from transaction type to history sheet group to history sheet version to a position within the history sheet, and finally to a column within the position, allows you to create the most powerful custom asset report imaginable, because you get to decide where and how all asset values will be displayed on your history sheet version.

> **Asset History Sheet Version Configuration Advice**
> If you still feel that the configuration of the Asset History Sheet Version is quite overwhelming, you're not alone. My advice is to simply start the configuration of your own Asset History Sheet Version and then process simple asset transactions one at a time. For example, configure the retirement columns in your custom version and then post one single retirement posting to see whether it shows up correctly in your report. Then repeat this process for all other positions in your report.

4.3 Chapter Summary

In this chapter, you learned that the Asset History Sheet report is by far the most important report at your disposal in Asset Accounting. The fact that you have complete control over the look, layout, and logic of this report makes it very unique and worthwhile, regardless of whether some configuration work is required. The important points to remember from this chapter are:

▶ **Asset History Sheet**
  This is by far the most important and powerful report available in Asset Accounting, because it combines the best features of balance-based and transaction-based reporting.

▶ **Custom Asset History Sheet versions**
  You should create your own custom Asset History Sheet versions to meet your company's specific reporting requirements. You can create as many versions as you need.

▶ **Configuration**
  The configuration for the Asset History Sheet version may seem complex in the beginning. Approach the configuration by testing small individual pieces of your version (i.e., configure the **Retirement** field first, and then test it by posting a retirement transaction). Breaking this process into small manageable pieces makes it much easier.

In Chapter 5, you'll learn about some of the specialty reports that are available in the standard Asset Accounting system. These reports are neither balance-based nor transaction-based reports; they simply provide additional asset reporting functions that you may find useful.

5 Specialty Reports

In this chapter, you'll learn about several specialty reports that you might find useful in your day-to-day operations, including the Barcode report (great tool for printing bar codes for asset tagging and tracking), the Physical Inventory List report (which helps with the physical inventory of fixed assets), the Asset Master Data Changes report (another great report to help you analyze who has changed what and when), and the Asset History report (not to be confused with the Asset History Sheet report discussed in Chapter 4). In addition, this chapter includes the following reports for specialty assets: Real Estate and Similar Rights report, Transportation Equipment report, Leasing report, and Insurance Value report.

5.1 Asset Barcode Report

The Asset Barcode report is a useful tool to produce barcode labels for certain fixed assets straight out of the standard SAP system. Tagging fixed assets with a barcode label allows for accurate tracking of equipment and can reduce lost items and overpayment of property taxes for items that you no longer own.

The information required to access the Asset Barcode report is as follows:

▶ **Menu Path**
  Accounting • Financial Accounting • Fixed Assets • Information System • Reports on Asset Accounting • Asset Balances • Inventory Lists • Bar Codes
▶ **Transaction Code**
  S_ALR_87010137
▶ **Technical Report Name**
  RABARC01

Main Report Purpose and Recipients

The Asset Barcode report is a simple asset listing, which includes the asset main number and subnumber, creation date, user, and description. The report does not include any asset values; it is used for asset tracking purposes. The main recipients of this report are general asset accounting departments.

The Selection Screen

Figure 5.1 shows the selection screen for the Asset Barcode report. It is a very simplistic version of the basic selection screen with which you are already familiar. You'll notice that this report doesn't include a reporting date or depreciation area field. These fields aren't necessary because the report doesn't include any asset values.

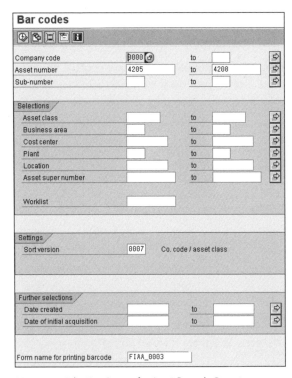

Figure 5.1 Selection Screen for Asset Barcode Report

One difference from the standard selection screen is that in the **Further selections** area, fields for the **Date created** and **Date of initial acquisition** are included. This makes it easy to run the report on a periodic basis and only include assets that have been acquired in the last quarter, for example.

The selection screen also includes a field for the **Form name for printing barcode**. This field refers to a SAPscript form, which controls the actual layout of the barcode label and the information that is included on the label. SAP delivers a standard form FIAA_0003 as a good example for a barcode label, but you're free to create your own labels. You can use the Form Painter (Transaction **SE71**) to modify the existing form or even create a new form.

Report Output

Figure 5.2 shows the standard report output of the Asset Barcode report. As you can see, it is a very basic asset list. The only difference this report compared to the standard asset report output is the button labeled **Print barcodes**.

Once you have selected the assets you want to tag with barcode labels, simply click **Print barcodes** and the report will print the actual barcode labels according to the design of the SAPscript form you entered on the selection screen.

Capturing Asset Information with Third-Party Tools

Once you have tagged your assets with barcodes, you can use any of the third-party software tools available to capture the asset information during regular inventories and transfer the information back into the SAP system.

> **Barcode solution providers**
>
> I have compiled this short list of barcode solution providers as a reference for you. For more information, please read OSS note 172251.
>
> ▶ Data Systems International
>   *www.dsionline.com*
> ▶ Freudenberg IT
>   *www.freudenberg-it.de*
> ▶ TIG International
>   *www.tigint.com*
> ▶ Sage Data
>   *www.sagedata.com*

5.2 Physical Inventory List Report

Because we just discussed the Asset Barcode report, it makes sense to now introduce you to the Physical Inventory List report. After you have tagged assets with barcodes, you would have to perform regular physical inventories to update the assets' locations in SAP and remove any records that can no longer be found or may have been disposed of.

Bar codes

	Print barcodes						
Report date:	12/31/2007	Bar codes			Creation date:	04/15/2007	1

CompanyCode 3000	AssetClass 4001		

Main number	SNo.	Date opend	Created by	Name	
4205	0	03/31/2005	BINSTOCK	Windows	
4206	0	03/31/2005	BINSTOCK	Doors	
4207	0	03/08/2007	M2B01	Building renovation	
4208	0	03/26/2007	M2B01	New Carpeting in Administration Bldg.	
AssetClass	4001			AuC for Measures	*
CompanyCode	3000			IDES US INC	**

Figure 5.2 Barcode Report Output

The information required to access the Physical Inventory List report is as follows:

- ▶ **Menu Path**
  Accounting • Financial Accounting • Fixed Assets • Information System • Reports on Asset Accounting • Asset Balances • Inventory Lists • Physical Inventory List
- ▶ **Transaction Code**
  S_ALR_87011979 thru S_ALR_87011982
- ▶ **Technical Report Name**
  Query – AM01

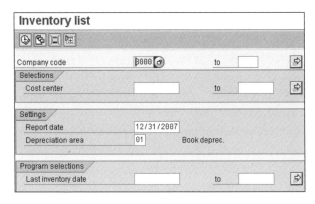

Figure 5.3 Selection Screen for Physical Inventory List Report

Main Report Purpose and Recipients

The Physical Inventory List report is a simple asset listing, which includes company code, plant, cost center and the asset's inventory number for identification purposes during physical inventories. The report also includes the asset description, acquisition year, and acquisition value, as well as asset quantity. The main recipients of this report are general asset accounting departments.

The Selection Screen

The Physical Inventory List report uses a simple selection screen with basic selection criteria. One noteworthy additional selection option, **Last inventory date,** is shown in Figure 5.3. This option allows you to run this report for assets that have been included in prior physical inventories. Alternatively, if you set the **Last inventory date** field to its initial value of 00/00/0000, you can run this report for assets that have never been inventoried before. This makes producing lists for rolling physical inventories a much simpler task.

Report Output

The actual inventory list is a simple asset listing by company code, plant, and cost center. An interesting feature of this report is that it shows the asset's inventory number by default (if no inventory number is stored in the asset master record, the report shows the asset main number and subnumber instead). Figure 5.4 shows the default report layout.

Specifying Assets to Include

It doesn't make sense to include every asset in an inventory list; for example, land and buildings wouldn't really have to be inventoried since they can't get lost or move locations. That's why you have to tell Asset Accounting specifically which assets you want to include in a physical inventory.

You do this by flagging each individual asset (typically, you would set this flag as a default value for the appropriate asset classes you want to include in an inventory).

Inventory list

CoCd	Plant	Cost center	Inventory number	Asset description	Acquisition value	Currency	Quantity	Un	Acq.	Remark
3000	3200	1810	3381 0000	PC - Maxitec 120xts	1,389.00	USD	1	PC	2004	
		1812	3379 0000	Company Car (Pontiac)	33,800.00	USD	1	PC	2004	
		1814	3380 0000	Company Car (Chrysler)	29,900.00	USD	1	PC	2004	

Figure 5.4 Physical Inventory List Report

Figure 5.5 shows the fields specifically used for this purpose, under the **Inventory** section on the first screen of the asset master record.

Figure 5.5 Inventory-Specific Fields on Asset Master Record

The option **Include asset in inventory list** must be selected for an asset to show up on the report. Additionally, you may add the **Last inventory on** date and an **Inventory note** to the asset master record after the asset has been updated.

5.3 Asset Master Data Changes Report

In general, the SAP system does a very good job of tracking changes made to any master records (e.g., G/L account master records, customers, vendors, fixed assets, etc.). These changes are stored in individual change documents and can be retrieved easily from the individual master record.

Sometimes, however, you're not interested in the changes for only one single asset master, but in the changes made to a range of assets, or changes made during a specific time frame, or made by a specific user. That's why SAP delivers the *Asset Master Data Changes* report, or as some people refer to it, the Asset Change Audit report. It is a very comprehensive listing of all asset master data changes that can be run for a date range by user ID, and even is limited to specific fields that have been changed. The information required to access the Asset Master Data Changes report is as follows:

> ▶ **Menu Path**
> **Accounting • Financial Accounting • Fixed Assets • Information System • Reports on Asset Accounting • Preparations for closing • International • Changes to Asset Master Records**
> ▶ **Transaction Code**
> **S_ALR_87012037**
> ▶ **Technical Report Name**
> **RAAEND01**

Main Report Purpose and Recipients

The Asset Master Data Changes report is a comprehensive change report that lists all master data changes, including old and new information, and user, date, and time information to provide an audit trail for all asset master and value changes. The main recipients of this report are general asset accounting, tax, and internal controls departments.

The Selection Screen

Figure 5.6 shows the selection screen for this report. Note the **Further selections** section, where you can limit the report by **Date of change**, **Changed by (name)**, and **Field changed**.

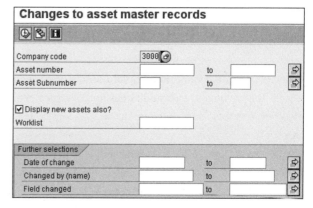

Figure 5.6 Asset Master Data Changes Report Selection Screen

One interesting feature of this report is the option **Display new assets also?** When an asset master is created, the system writes a change document even though no actual change has taken place. You can exclude these pseudo-changes by clearing the **Display new assets also ?** option.

Limiting the Report to a Specific Field

When you want to limit the report to a specific field that was changed, you have to enter the technical field name in the option **Field changed.**

> **Example**
> In Figure 5.7, I entered the technical field name **AFASL** (which is the Depreciation key on the asset master record) to get a list of all assets where this field was changed. I also entered my own user ID to limit this report to assets that I have changed.

Figure 5.7 Selection by Technical Field Name

Report Output

Figure 5.8 shows the basic report output. The report shows the information regarding the change, including the following:

▶ Date/Time of the change

▶ User who performed the change

▶ Asset number (here: **1113-0**)

▶ Object that was changed (column **AttrDescr**: Depreciation key)

▶ Before and after values in the columns **Old Value** and **New Value**

Also shown is the column **EnhObjVal** (Enhanced Object Value). This column shows additional metadata for the actual object that was changed. In this example, the depreciation key was changed. The question now is what depreciation area it was changed in. You'll find the answer in the Enhanced Object Value column (**EnhObjVal**) – depreciation area 10 was changed.

Possible Uses

In my career as a consultant, I have found this report to be very useful when analyzing asset value problems. For example, clients would call me saying that their depreciation values had changed inexplicably. After running this report, I was able to quickly identify why depreciation values had changed, as well as be able to determine who changed them.

5.4 Asset History Report

Usually, when people want to print asset information – be it asset master record information or asset values – they resort to taking screenshots and inserting them into Microsoft Word documents. There is a much more elegant way to do this however. This is where the *Asset History* report comes in. As its name implies, it provides a complete picture of an asset's history, including all master record information as well as asset values.

Caution

Do not confuse this report with the Asset History Sheet report!

The information required to access the Asset History report is as follows:

▶ **Menu Path**
Accounting • Financial Accounting • Fixed Assets • Information System • Reports on Asset Accounting • History • Asset History

▶ **Transaction Code**
S_ALR_87012075

▶ **Technical Report Name**
RAHIST01

Main Report Purpose and Recipients

The Asset History report is a comprehensive report that includes all asset master record fields and values. The main recipients of this report are general asset accounting departments.

The Selection Screen

Figure 5.9 shows the selection screen for this report. As you can see, it is an abbreviated version of the basic selection screen.

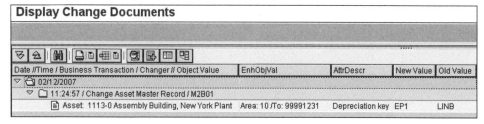

Figure 5.8 Asset Change Document with Old and New Values

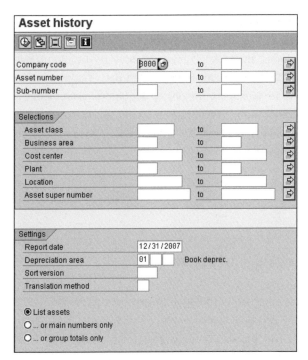

Figure 5.9   Asset History Report Selection Screen

Customizing the Report

The neat thing about this report is that the output is driven by a SAPscript form (similar to the Barcode report we discussed in Section 5.1), which means that you can customize the report output yourself simply by modifying the SAPscript form. You can decide what information to include or exclude from the report and how to display the information.

Assigning the SAPscript Form to Each Asset Class

Once you have set up the SAPscript form, you have to assign it to each asset class in configuration (Transaction **OAAY**) as shown in Figure 5.10. You also could decide that you need multiple different asset history forms for different asset classes since the information included in each would vary by asset class (i.e., you might include the field License Plate Number for asset class Autos & Trucks while not including it in the Buildings asset class).

Class	Asset class description	Layout set name
1000	Real estate	FIAA_F001
1010		
1100	Buildings	FIAA_F001
2000	Machines declining depr.	FIAA_F001
2100	Machines straight-line-depr.	FIAA_F001

Figure 5.10   Assign a Layout Set to Each Asset Class

The Standard SAPscript

SAP delivers standard SAPscript form FIAA_F001 for the Asset History report, which you can use as a template to develop your own version.

Report Output

Figure 5.11 shows the screen output of the Asset History report. The standard SAPscript layout includes just about all asset master record and value fields, making this report several pages long for just one single asset. You may decide to narrow down your layout to include just a certain range of fields, which are actually being used in your system instead. This will make the report far more manageable for you.

```
                          A S S E T   C H A R T

Asset                              3329-0   IBM Thinkpad 770
Class                              3200     Personal computers
Company code                       3000


                            Master data

General data
Description              IBM Thinkpad 770


Acct. allocation    30000 Fixtures and fittings
Inventory number
Quantity                              1  EA

Inventory
Last inventory on
Inventory note

Posting information
Capitalized on                          Deactivation on
First acquis. on                        Planned retmt. on
Acquis. period                   / 000 Ordered on

Time-dep.data from 01/01/1900 to 12/31/9999
Business area                    9900
Cost center                      SRB100
Activity type
Internal order
Work order

Plant
Location
Room
Tax jurisd. code         0508127901
License plate no.
```

Figure 5.11   Asset History Report Output

Typically, you would run this report for a single asset or a small range of assets only, in order to provide the report recipient with a detailed overview and history for an asset (i.e., an auditor may ask for a complete asset picture). This report provides a very nice alternative to taking screenshots.

5.5 Real Estate and Similar Rights Report

SAP specifically designed the *Real Estate and Similar Rights* report to use with real property assets such as real estate holdings and land, because these assets are subject to property tax payments to the local tax assessor's office. You can store the corresponding information in the individual asset's master record and retrieve it by using this report.

The information required to access the Real Estate and Similar Rights report is as follows:

- ▶ **Menu Path**
  Accounting • Financial Accounting • Fixed Assets • Information System • Reports on Asset Accounting • Asset Balances • Real Estate and Similar Rights
- ▶ **Transaction Code**
  S_ALR_87010127
- ▶ **Technical Report Name**
  Query/AM02

Main Report Purpose and Recipients

This report is intended to show real property assets, their associated values, and related information from the tax assessor's office. The main recipients of this report are general asset accounting and tax accounting departments.

The Selection Screen

The Real Estate and Similar Rights report is an ABAP query report, and therefore it uses a version of the basic selection screen that is shared by all query-based reports. Because this report can be used for local municipality reporting for property tax purposes, this report includes two selection fields for the **Local tax office** and **Municipality**, as shown in Figure 5.12. This makes it easy to create reports for the individual local tax assessor's office.

Figure 5.12 Real Estate-Specific Selection Criteria

Report Output

Figure 5.13 shows the default report output, which includes the asset's acquisition year, the municipality it belongs to, the area covered (i.e., if applicable for land for example), the posted acquisition value, and the assessed value as determined by the tax assessor's office. Typically, the assessed value is the basis for property tax payments.

Class	Asset	SN	Description	Acq.	Municipality	Area	Σ Acquisition value	Σ Assessed value
1100	1105	0	Warehouse	1993	Houston	1,254.000	414,033.50	500,500.00
	1106	0	Office Building	1993	Dallas	22,225.000	9,970,191.68	240,807.88
	1106	1	Office Addition	1998	Dallas	1,000.000	5,368,564.75	6,000,000.00
1100							15,752,789.93	6,741,307.88
							15,752,789.93	6,741,307.88

Figure 5.13 Real Estate Report

The information shown in this report can be entered on the individual asset's master record. Figure 5.14 shows the **Net Worth Tax** tab with the real estate fields of an asset included.

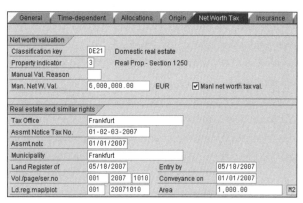

Figure 5.14 Real Estate Information in the Asset Master Record

Tip

Tax departments are responsible for correct tax payments, including property taxes, and they have an interest in keeping tax payments to a minimum.

Downloading the Real Estate and Similar Rights report to Microsoft Excel, and adding a column that calculates the difference between actual acquisition cost and assessed value can help you to identify assets with large discrepancies between these two numbers. These assets can then be analyzed for a possible reduction in assessed values, thereby providing an opportunity for lowering tax payments.

5.6 Transportation Equipment Report

SAP specifically designed the *Transportation Equipment* report for transportation equipment assets such as automobiles, trucks, and other vehicles. Vehicle-specific information, such as the license plate number, can be stored in the asset master record and is shown on this report.

The information required to access the Transportation Equipment report is as follows:

▶ **Menu Path**
Accounting • Financial Accounting • Fixed Assets • Information System • Reports on Asset Accounting • Asset Balances • Transportation Equipment
▶ **Transaction Code**
S_ALR_87010129
▶ **Technical Report Name**
Query/AM03

Main Report Purpose and Recipients

This report is intended to show vehicles and their associated values and related information. The main recipients of this report are general asset accounting and fleet management departments.

The Selection Screen

The Transportation Equipment report is an ABAP query report. Therefore, it uses a version of the basic selection screen, which is shared by all query-based reports. Because company-owned vehicles can be assigned to specific employees, the selection screen includes a field for the **Personnel Number**. Furthermore, vehicles are typically managed by a central fleet management department and therefore, the selection screen includes a field for the **Cost center** (or department). Figure 5.15 shows both of these selection fields.

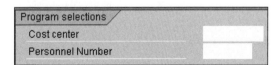

Figure 5.15 Personnel Number Selection

Report Output

Figure 5.16 shows the default report output, which includes the asset's acquisition year, **License plate num-**

ber, **Vendor** number of the vendor from whom the vehicle was purchased, as well as the **Acquisition value** (cost) and current **Book value**.

Vehicles							
Asset	SN	Description	Acq.	License plate number	Vendor	Σ Acquisition value	Σ Book value
3104	0	VW Golf GL	1994	HD-MR 906	1100	24,109.95	5,923.00
3105	0	VW Passat	1994	HD-JA 3425	1100	29,457.08	7,494.00
3107	0	Ford Mondeo	1994	HD-JG 7485	1100	22,863.70	2,272.00
					■	76,430.73 ■	15,689.00

Figure 5.16 Vehicle Report Default Layout

You can enter both the **License plate number** and **Personnel Number** used by this report on the individual asset's master record. Figure 5.17 shows these fields as they appear on the **Time-dependent Data** tab.

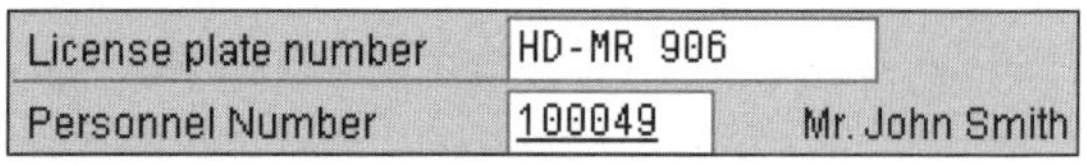

License plate number	HD-MR 906	
Personnel Number	100049	Mr. John Smith

Figure 5.17 Vehicle Information in Asset Master Record

5.7 Leasing Report

SAP specifically designed the *Leasing* report for leased assets. Leasing information such as the lease start date and length, the leasing company and agreement number, as well as leasing payment information, can be stored in the asset master record and is then displayed on this report.

The information required to access the **Leasing** report is as follows:

▶ **Menu Path**
Accounting • Financial Accounting • Fixed Assets • Information System • Reports on Asset Accounting • Asset Balances • Leased Assets • Leasing
▶ **Transaction Code**
S_ALR_87010139
▶ **Technical Report Name**
Query/AM04

Main Report Purpose and Recipients

This report is intended to show information related to leased assets. The main recipients of this report are general asset accounting and fleet management, or Information Technology (IT) departments (for leased vehicles or leased computer equipment).

The Selection Screen

The Leasing report is an ABAP query report. Therefore, it uses a version of the basic selection screen that is shared by all query-based reports. This report includes two leasing-specific selection fields: **Leasing company** and **Lease start date**. Figure 5.18 shows both of these selection fields.

Figure 5.18 Leasing-Specific Selection Criteria

Report Output

Figure 5.19 shows the default report output that includes the leasing agreement number, leasing company, leasing start date, lease length, and payment. The specific leasing information shown in this report can be entered on the individual asset's master record. Figure 5.20 shows the **Leasing** tab with these fields.

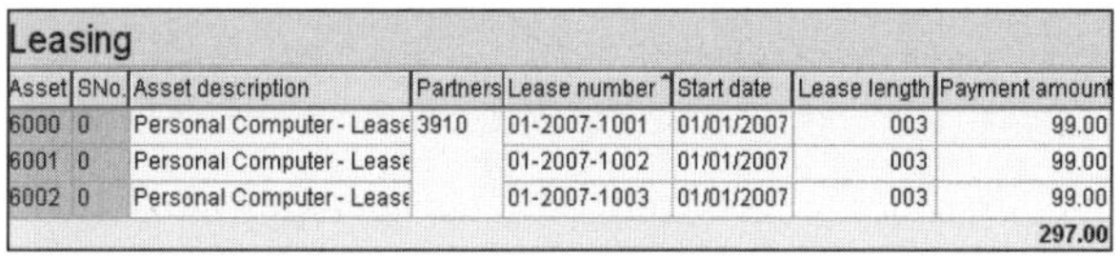

Leasing						
Asset	SNo.	Asset description	Partners	Lease number	Start date	Lease length	Payment amount
6000	0	Personal Computer - Lease	3910	01-2007-1001	01/01/2007	003	99.00
6001	0	Personal Computer - Lease		01-2007-1002	01/01/2007	003	99.00
6002	0	Personal Computer - Lease		01-2007-1003	01/01/2007	003	99.00
							297.00

Figure 5.19 Leasing Report Default Output

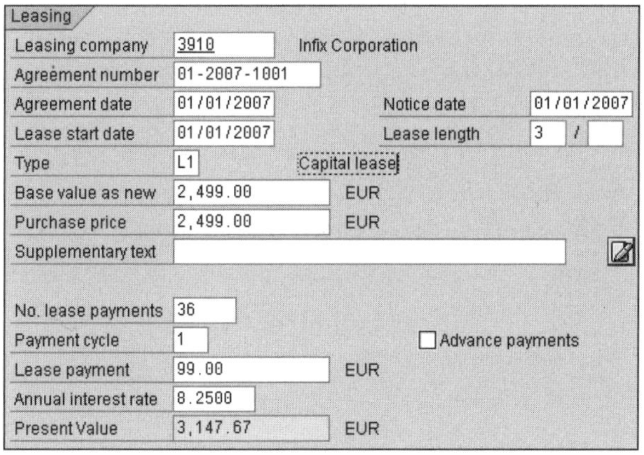

Leasing				
Leasing company	3910	Infix Corporation		
Agreement number	01-2007-1001			
Agreement date	01/01/2007	Notice date	01/01/2007	
Lease start date	01/01/2007	Lease length	3	/
Type	L1	Capital lease		
Base value as new	2,499.00	EUR		
Purchase price	2,499.00	EUR		
Supplementary text				
No. lease payments	36			
Payment cycle	1	☐ Advance payments		
Lease payment	99.00	EUR		
Annual interest rate	8.2500			
Present Value	3,147.67	EUR		

Figure 5.20 Leasing Information in Asset Master Record

5.8 Insurance Values Report

Companies typically insure their fixed assets against loss, theft, damage, or other perils. They may self-insure for these risks or purchase insurance policies from third-party insurance providers. In the latter case, companies would typically store certain insurance-related information in the asset master record and use the *Insurance Values* report to produce a report that can then be used to calculate insurance premiums.

The information required to access the Insurance Values report is as follows:

▶ **Menu Path**
  Accounting • Financial Accounting • Fixed Assets • Information System • Reports on Asset Accounting • Specific Valuations • International • Insurance Values

▶ **Transaction Code**
  S_ALR_87012030

▶ **Technical Report Name**
  RAVERS_ALV01

Main Report Purpose and Recipients

This report is intended to show insurance information for assets. The main recipients of this report are general asset accounting departments, risk management groups, and insurance carriers.

The Selection Screen

The Insurance Values report uses a version of the basic selection screen with some minor additions. Figure 5.21 shows that the **Further selections** section includes the following insurance-specific fields:

▶ **Insurance type**
  The insurance type defines control features for the insurance settings in the Asset Accounting configuration and can be used to differentiate between different insurance types (such as fire insurance, automobile insurance, etc.)

▶ **Insurance company**
  The insurance company refers to the company that provides the insurance coverage.

▶ **Insurance index series**
  The index series is usually published by insurance companies and is used to calculate the replacement value for an asset.

▶ **Insurable value**
  You can manually specify an insurable value for an asset instead of having the system calculate one. If

you manually specify an insurable value, you can use this field for report selection.

▶ **Base insurable value**
This field refers to the base value for the insurance calculation (typically, the base insurable value can either be the asset's acquisition cost with or without prior year price increases).

Further selections			
Balance sheet account		to	
Capitalization date		to	
Insurance type		to	
Insurance company		to	
Insurance index series		to	
Insurable value		to	
Base insurable value		to	

Figure 5.21 Insurance-Specific Selection Fields

Report Output

Figure 5.22 shows the default report output that includes the insurance start date and agreement number, as well as the insurance values. The insurance information used by this report can be entered on the individual asset's master record. Figure 5.23 shows the **Insurance** section with these fields.

Asset	SNo.	Cap.date	Asset description	Start date	Agreement no.	Suppl. text	Σ	Ins.val.	Σ	Base ins. val.	Σ	Acquis.val.
6001	0	05/18/2007	Personal Computer - Leased	01/01/2007	001-110-2007	Standard Insurance Policy		1,665.00		0.00		2,499.00
Insur.Companies 01							▪	**1,665.00**	▪	**0.00**	▪	**2,499.00**
6002	0	05/18/2007	Personal Computer - Leased	03/01/2007	031-115-2007	Standard Insurance Policy		1,665.00		0.00		2,499.00
Insur.Companies 02							▪	**1,665.00**	▪	**0.00**	▪	**2,499.00**
Type 02							▪▪	**3,330.00**	▪▪	**0.00**	▪▪	**4,998.00**

Figure 5.22 Insurance Value Default Report Layout

Insurance		
Type	02	Current value insurance
Insur.Companies	02	MG & Partner Insurance
Agreement number	031-115-2007	
Suppl. text	Standard Insurance Policy	
Start date	03/01/2007	
Insurance rate	1002	Normal premium
Index series	00070	Office Machines/Data Processing Products
Base value	0.00	EUR ☐ Manual Update
		FYear Change
Man.insur.val.		EUR per
Curr. Ins. Val.	1,665.00	EUR per 2007

Figure 5.23 Insurance Information on an Asset Master Record

5.9 Chapter Summary

This chapter introduced you to some of the lesser known or specialty reports available in Asset Accounting, which are summarized here:

- **Asset Barcode Report**

  This report can print barcode labels for the assets you include. The actual barcode label can be configured according to your requirements using the SAPscript functionality.

- **Physical Inventory List Report**

  Once assets have been tagged (via barcode or other means), you should run periodic physical inventories. This report helps you with this task by listing all assets that you want to include in such an inventory (you include assets by setting the corresponding flag in the asset master record).

- **Asset Master Data Changes Report**

  This is an audit report for fixed assets that shows all changes made to assets. The report can be limited to certain date ranges, user IDs, or specific asset fields that were changed, and it includes the old and new values.

- **Asset History Report**

  This little-known report provides an elegant way for you to print the entire history for an asset master record, including the asset master record fields and asset values. The actual output of the report can be customized to meet your specific requirements using the SAPscript functionality. Do not confuse this report with the Asset History Sheet report discussed earlier in Chapter 4.

- **Real Estate and Similar Rights Report**

  Use this report to report specific information related to real property assets such as buildings, land, and other real estate holdings.

- **Transportation Equipment Report**

  Use this report to show vehicle values including unique information such as license plate numbers and personnel numbers of the employee assigned the vehicle.

- **Leasing Report**

  This report was designed for leased assets and includes information about the individual leasing arrangement, specifically the lease agreement number, start date, as well as lease length and lease payment.

- **Insurance Values Report**

  The Insurance Value report is used to show insurance replacement values for individual assets, and includes additional insurance-specific information such as insurance agreement number and insurance policy start date.

Looking ahead, in Chapter 6, we'll discuss reports designed specifically for U.S. tax reporting purposes.

6 US Tax Reports

While SAP is certainly not in the business of providing local tax expertise around the world, it does deliver a range of reports specifically designed to address US Tax reporting requirements. These reports will not print the actual US Tax forms, but they will provide the information necessary to complete and file these tax forms.

In this chapter, you'll learn about the specific US Tax reports available. Keep in mind that SAP delivers several other tax-related reports for countries other than the US. Typically, if a particular report is a local, legal requirement, SAP delivers a report to address the issue.

> **Note**
> This chapter does not provide any legal tax advice or recommendations. For that information, you should see your tax professional.

6.1 Mid-Quarter Alert Report

Usually, all personal property starts to depreciate at the middle of the fiscal year for tax purposes (so called *half-year convention*). If, however, a company purchased 40% of all current year acquisitions in the last fiscal quarter, the mid-quarter convention rule comes into play. It requires that the depreciation start date for each asset be changed from the middle of the fiscal year to the middle of the fiscal quarter that the asset was acquired in.

For example, if you acquired an asset on 3/31 of the fiscal year, the depreciation start date would be set to 7/1 following the half-year convention. If you now have to switch to a mid-quarter convention, the start date must be changed to 2/16, because that is the middle of the first fiscal quarter.

> **Tip**
> Many people make the mistake of setting the start date to the 15th of the month. This is, however, not accurate, because the 16th is the first day of the second half of the month.

The *Mid-Quarter Alert* report in Asset Accounting helps you with this issue by determining what the percentage of acquisitions is for each fiscal quarter and whether you fall over or under the 40% rule. Once you are over the rule, you must apply the depreciation start date changes and corresponding depreciation value recalculations.

The information required to access the Mid-Quarter Alert report is as follows:

▶ **Menu Path**
  Accounting • Financial Accounting • Fixed Assets • Information System • Reports on Asset Accounting • Preparations for Closing • Country Specifics • USA • Asset Acquisitions (Mid-Quarter-Convention)
▶ **Transaction Code**
  S_ALR_87012047
▶ **Technical Report Name**
  RAUSMQ10

Main Report Purpose and Recipients

The Mid-Quarter Alert report shows acquisitions by fiscal quarter to calculate the acquisition percentage as required by the mid-quarter convention. The main recipients for this report are tax departments.

The Selection Screen

Figure 6.1 shows the selection screen for this report. As you can see, it is similar to the selection screen for the

Depreciation Simulation report we discussed in Chapter 2. The Mid-Quarter Alert report can forecast asset acquisitions by taking into account existing capital investment measures, such as internal orders, WBS elements, investment programs and positions, and even appropriation requests. The forecasted acquisitions are based on the depreciation simulation data you have entered in the master records of the investment measures. For the report to base its forecast on planned or budgeted values, select the checkbox **Dep. simul. based on budget** in the section **Planned cap. investments**.

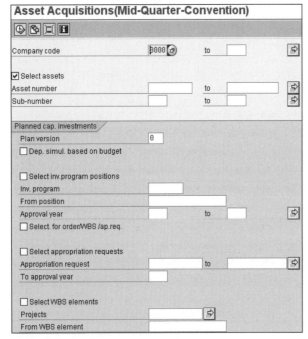

Figure 6.1 Mid-Quarter Alert Selection Screen

When to Include and Exclude Capital Investment Measures

If you run the Mid-Quarter Alert report for the current year to forecast whether your company will be in or close to a mid-quarter alert situation, be sure to include the existing capital investment measures (internal orders, WBS elements, appropriation requests, investment pro-

gram positions) in this report. This will produce the most accurate Mid-Quarter Alert report possible, assuming that you have maintained the depreciation simulation data on the investment measures.

If, however, you run this report for a prior, already closed fiscal year, you normally wouldn't include the investment measures because all actual settlements have already taken place. In this case, you don't want to include planned capital investments because the year has already been closed.

Report Output

The report output shown in Figure 6.2 shows all asset acquisitions by the sort level of the selected sort version and divided into each fiscal quarter. Note that this example uses sort version 0007 (sorted and subtotaled by asset class).

Also notice that the report issued an error message under the **Message** column header. It indicates that the mid-quarter alert convention rule (at least 40% of acquisitions in the fourth quarter) has already been exceeded for this particular class.

Avoiding the Mid-Quarter Convention

The column labeled **Max. amt. acc. to MQC** (Maximum amount according to mid-quarter convention) shows the *safe* amount you can still capitalize in the fourth quarter without triggering the mid-quarter alert. This is a very useful number to know when you plan your final year-end settlements and want to avoid the mid-quarter convention. Simply make sure that your capitalizations in the fourth quarter stay under the amount shown.

Including Prior Year Transactions

It is important to realize that the acquisitions shown in this report are based on SAP's standard determination of asset acquisitions, which exclude current year settlements from prior year investment measures. For example, say you started an internal order last year and spent

All. object types	Σ	1st Quarter	Σ	2nd Quarter	Σ	3rd Quarter	Σ	4th Quarter	Σ	All Quarters	Σ	Max. amt. acc. to MQC	;	Crcy	Message
Asset	⬈	0.00		0.00		118,470.00		209,140.00		327,610.00		78,980.00		USD	MQC total is already exceeded
Asset Class 2100	▪	0.00	▪	0.00	▪	118,470.00	▪	209,140.00	▪	327,610.00	▪	78,980.00		USD	
Asset		100,886.00		0.00		12,600.00		39,950.00		153,436.00		75,657.33		USD	
Asset Class 3200	▪	100,886.00	▪	0.00	▪	12,600.00	▪	39,950.00	▪	153,436.00	▪	75,657.33		USD	
Company Code 3000	▪▪	100,886.00	▪▪	0.00	▪▪	131,070.00	▪▪	249,090.00	▪▪	481,046.00	▪▪	154,637.33		USD	

Figure 6.2 Mid-Quarter Alert Report Output

$10,000 for capital items. At the end of the year, the project wasn't completed yet and therefore, the order was settled to the corresponding Asset under Construction (AuC) or Construction in Progress account. In the current year, you spent another $5,000 for additional capital items, and then performed a full settlement of the order to the final fixed asset.

The final asset will show an acquisition amount of $15,000, but this amount was posted using two different transaction types (one indicating that the spending occurred in a previous year, and the other indicating current year spending). The Mid-Quarter Alert report will include only the current year spending, because it considers the prior year amount a transfer between assets and not an acquisition.

Note

To change the logic of this report to include such prior year transactions, you have to implement the coding changes described in OSS note 770263.

6.2 Total Depreciation Report for Form 4562

Although we've already discussed the *Total Depreciation* report in Chapter 2, there's a brief review here because of the relevance of this report to tax reporting.

The information required to access the Total Depreciation report is as follows:

▶ **Menu Path**
Accounting • Financial Accounting • Fixed Assets • Information System • Reports on Asset Accounting • Explanation for P&L • International • Depreciation • Total Depreciation

▶ **Transaction Code**
S_ALR_87012004

▶ **Technical Report Name**
RAHAFA_ALV01

Main Report Purpose and Recipients

The Total Depreciation report is a comprehensive asset listing, which can be used as the main tax report for IRS form 4562 when used with a proper sort version. The main recipients of this report are tax accounting departments.

IRS Form 4562

One of the main IRS tax forms is 4562, which essentially shows the depreciation amounts for assets grouped by useful life (see Figure 6.3 for that part of the actual form). The standard SAP system does not include a sort version by useful life, so it is important for you to create one during configuration. Chapter 1 discussed the details for setting up custom sort versions.

In order to make filling out the IRS form 4562 as easy as possible, you need subtotals by useful life. Figure 6.4 shows the Total Depreciation report sorted and subtotaled by **Asset Class** and **Useful life**. This makes it easy

Section B—Assets Placed in Service During 2006 Tax Year Using the General Depreciation System						
(a) Classification of property	(b) Month and year placed in service	(c) Basis for depreciation (business/investment use only—see instructions)	(d) Recovery period	(e) Convention	(f) Method	(g) Depreciation deduction
19a 3-year property						
b 5-year property						
c 7-year property						
d 10-year property						
e 15-year property						
f 20-year property						
g 25-year property			25 yrs.		S/L	
h Residential rental property			27.5 yrs.	MM	S/L	
			27.5 yrs.	MM	S/L	
i Nonresidential real property			39 yrs.	MM	S/L	
				MM	S/L	
Section C—Assets Placed in Service During 2006 Tax Year Using the Alternative Depreciation System						
20a Class life					S/L	
b 12-year			12 yrs.		S/L	
c 40-year			40 yrs.	MM	S/L	

Figure 6.3 IRS Form 4562 – Depreciation by Useful Life (Source: www.irs.gov)

Depreciation

CoCode	Asset Class		Useful life	Σ	Cum.acq.value	Σ	Accum.dep.	Σ	Start book.val	Σ	PIndDep
3000	1000	🖫		▪	64,252,236.00	▪	0.00	▪	64,252,236.00	▪	0.00
	1100		39		3,188,883.00		910,881.00-		2,278,002.00		81,767.00-
			50		84,546,755.48		25,934,064.48-		58,612,691.00		1,805,784.00-
	1100	🖫		▪	87,735,638.48	▪	26,844,945.48-	▪	60,890,693.00	▪	1,887,551.00-
	2000		7		9,748,259.24		9,660,672.24-		87,587.00		25,025.00-
			10		4,000.00		4,000.00-		0.00		0.00
	2000	🖫		▪	9,752,259.24	▪	9,664,672.24-	▪	87,587.00	▪	25,025.00-
	2100		7		3,086,484.39		2,944,747.39-		141,737.00		47,831.00-
	2100	🖫		▪	3,086,484.39	▪	2,944,747.39-	▪	141,737.00	▪	47,831.00-

Figure 6.4 Total Depreciation Report Subtotaled by Useful Life

for users to copy the depreciation amounts directly into form 4562. Without an appropriate sort version, users would have to add up the depreciation amounts manually in a Microsoft Excel sheet.

6.3 Depreciation Comparison Report

Another useful report for the tax department is the *Depreciation Comparison* report. It lets users compare up to three depreciation areas simultaneously. The report will show the values in each individual depreciation area and then calculate the differences between them automatically.

The information required to access the Depreciation Comparison report is as follows:

▶ **Menu Path**
Accounting • Financial Accounting • Fixed Assets • Information System • Reports on Asset Accounting • Explanation for P&L • International • Depreciation Comparison
▶ **Transaction Code**
S_ALR_87012013
▶ **Technical Report Name**
RABIKA_ALV01

Main Report Purpose and Recipients
The Depreciation Comparison report enables you to compare up to three depreciation areas simultaneously. The main recipients of this report are tax accounting departments.

The Selection Screen
Figure 6.5 shows the selection screen for the Depreciation Comparison report. It is a version of the basic selection screen with two noteworthy additions. Where you usually see only one field for the **Depreciation area**, the report now lets you enter up to three areas (you can enter only two areas as well).

Furthermore, you can include all assets in this report or limit the report to only assets where differences between the depreciation areas exist, as shown in Figure 6.6. It's important to note that these differences refer to differences in depreciation amounts and not to differences in acquisition costs.

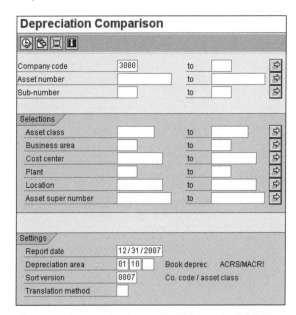

Figure 6.5 Depreciation Comparison Report Selection Screen

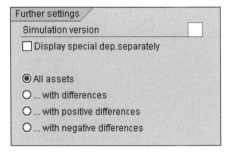

Figure 6.6 Include All Assets or Just Assets with Differences

Report Output

Figure 6.7 shows the basic report output when comparing two depreciation areas. This report can be used by tax departments to perform depreciation comparisons between book and tax depreciation, and depreciation comparisons between Federal Tax and Alternative Minimum Tax (AMT) books.

Caveats

Notice that the report shows all value columns with the same description. For example, the report shows two columns titled **Acquis. val.** This is an unfortunate oversight from a development perspective. Therefore, it is important to understand that the value columns correspond to the order of the depreciation areas as they were entered on the selection screen.

Unfortunately, this information is lost when someone prints or saves the report. Should you choose to save the report, I would recommend that you include the depreciation area information in the description of the file name.

6.4 Analysis of Retirement Revenue Report

Tax departments must report ordinary versus capital gains or losses at the end of the year from asset retirements. The term *ordinary* refers to all asset retirements where the asset was held less than one year.

If an asset was held for more than one year and then was retired, the transaction would result in capital gains or losses. These gains and losses must be separated by real property vs. personal property. Real property refers to assets such as land or buildings, while personal property can be defined as any asset that can be moved. SAP's Asset Accounting provides the *Analysis of Retirement Revenue* report for this purpose.

The information required to access the Analysis of Retirement Revenue report is as follows:

- ▶ **Menu Path**
  Accounting • Financial Accounting • Fixed Assets • Information System • Reports on Asset Accounting • Taxes • Country Specifics • USA • Analysis of Retirement Revenue
- ▶ **Transaction Code**
  S_ALR_87012066
- ▶ **Technical Report Name**
  RAUSAG_ALV04

Main Report Purpose and Recipients

The Analysis of Retirement Revenue report is designed specifically for tax purposes to calculate capital gains and losses for real versus personal property assets. The main recipients of this report are tax accounting departments.

Depreciation Comparison

CoCd			Class		Σ	Acquis.val.	Σ	Acquis.val.	Σ	Plnd.ODep	Σ	Plnd.ODep	Σ	Book value	Σ	Book value	Σ Diff.pld.dep
3000	01	10	1000	Real estate		64,252,236.00		64,252,236.00		0.00		0.00		64,252,236.00		64,252,236.00	0.00
	01	10	1100	Buildings		87,735,638.48		87,735,638.48		1,869,562.00-		1,887,551.00-		58,852,108.00		59,003,142.00	17,989.00-
	01	10	2000	Machines decl. depr.		9,752,259.24		9,752,259.24		50,261.00-		25,025.00-		140,195.00		62,562.00	25,236.00
	01	10	2100	Machines str.-line		3,086,484.39		3,086,484.39		80,486.00-		47,831.00-		280,138.00		93,906.00	32,655.00
	01	10	3000	Fixture and fitting		435,183.69		435,183.69		900.00-		519.00		337.00		259.00	381.00
	01	10	3100	Vehicles		2,342,275.13		2,342,275.13		22,726.00-		13,090.00-		22,726.00		19,635.00	9,636.00
	01	10	3200	Personal computers		485,439.91		485,439.91		7,833.00-		4,145.00-		2,660.00		2,228.00	3,688.00
	01	10	4001	AuC for Measures		0.00		0.00		0.00		0.00		0.00		0.00	0.00
3000					▪	168,089,516.84	▪	168,089,516.84	▪	2,031,768.00-	▪	1,978,161.00-	▪	123,550,400.00	▪	123,433,968.00	▪ 53,607.00

Figure 6.7 Depreciation Comparison Report Layout

The Selection Screen

The selection screen for the Analysis of Retirement Revenue report is a version of the basic selection screen. There is only one noteworthy difference shown in Figure 6.8, namely, the field **Asset class real prop. (set)**.

Figure 6.8 Enter Set for Asset Classes

Since the report is supposed to separate capital gains and losses from ordinary gains and losses by asset type (real vs. personal assets), it needs to know what asset classes these real assets exist in. You can use the **Asset class real prop. (set)** field to enter a set name. Note that a *set* is a simple grouping of an SAP object, which in this case is the asset class.

> **Note**
>
> You can create sets using Transaction **GS01**, or Transaction **GS02** to edit an existing set. Figure 6.9 shows a sample basic set I created. Included are asset classes **1000** (which represents **Land** assets) and **1100** (which represents **Buildings**) in set **FIAA-001** to correspond to my real property assets. When I get ready to run this report, I simply enter the set name "FIAA-001" in the **Asset class real prop. (set)** field shown in Figure 6.8.

> **Tip**
>
> The **Asset class real prop. (set)** field does not have any input help (in the form of a drop-down icon or F4 input help) like all other fields in SAP. In other words, you must know the name of the corresponding set before you can run this report.

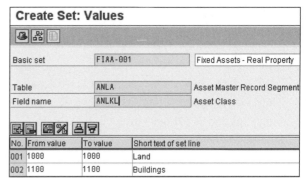

Figure 6.9 Create Set for Real Property Asset Classes

Report Output

Figure 6.10 shows the default report output of this report. Notice that it includes separate columns for the capital gains or losses, as well as the ordinary gains and losses.

If the asset is a real property asset as defined by the set used in the report, a capital gain/loss is converted to an ordinary gain/loss.

6.5 Net Worth Valuation (Property Tax) Report

Property taxes in the US are paid to the local tax authorities and are typically based on the net value of the assets within the taxing authorities' territory. Under certain circumstances, a local tax authority may decide to give property tax abatements to encourage businesses to expand or relocate to its community. In such cases, the property tax will be based on a value other than the net value.

The *Net Worth Valuation* report can be used for these property tax requirements, because it can track an assets true net value as well as a property tax specific value that is not based on the actual cost or depreciation of an asset.

Analysis of Retirement Revenue

CoCd	Class		∑ Retirement	∑ Ret. book value	∑ Ret. revenue	∑ Capital gain	∑ Capital loss	∑ Ordinary loss	∑ Ordinary gain
1000	1000	Real estate	100.00-	100.00-	10.00	0.00	0.00	90.00	0.00
	3000	Fixture and fitting	10,000.00-	8,333.00-	0.00	0.00	0.00	8,333.00	0.00
1000			▪ 10,100.00- ▪	8,433.00- ▪	10.00 ▪	0.00 ▪	0.00 ▪	8,423.00 ▪	0.00

Figure 6.10 Analysis of Retirement Revenue Report Layout

The information required to access the Net Worth Valuation report is as follows:

> ▶ **Menu Path**
>   Accounting • Financial Accounting • Fixed Assets •
>   Information System • Reports on Asset Account-
>   ing • Specific Valuations • International • Net
>   Worth Valuation
> ▶ **Transaction Code**
>   S_ALR_87012028
> ▶ **Technical Report Name**
>   RAVERM_ALV01

Main Report Purpose and Recipients

The Net Worth Valuation report is used for property tax purposes. The report includes asset acquisition cost and book value, as well as a property tax value. The main recipients of this report are tax accounting departments.

The Selection Screen

The Net Worth Valuation report uses a slightly modified version of the basic selection screen with two noteworthy changes. First, although the report includes asset values, there is no field for the depreciation area on the selection screen. Figure 6.11 shows the **Settings** section where you would normally expect to see the depreciation area field.

Settings	
Report date	12/31/2007
Sort version	0004 Co. code / property classif. /asset
◉ List assets	
○ ... or group totals only	

Figure 6.11 No Depreciation Area Field on the Selection Screen

The reason for this seemingly missing functionality is that the report will only use the depreciation area that was specifically classified as the property tax area in configuration Transaction **AO31**. Figure 6.12 shows the assignment between company code and property tax depreciation area.

So, before you can use the Net Worth Valuation report, be sure to designate a depreciation area as the property tax area (typically you would use a tax depreciation area and not the book depreciation area for this).

CoCd	Company Name	Property	Name of depreciation area
3000	IDES US INC	10	Federal Tax ACRS/MACRS
3010	Euro Subsidiary - Belgium	63	Tax balance sheet
3050	IDES Subsiduary UK	15	Tax balance sheet

Figure 6.12 Designate Depreciation Area as Property Tax Area

Another difference from the standard selection screen is that the **Further selections** section includes fields that are specifically related to the net worth tax fields on the asset master record, as shown in Figure 6.13.

Further selections			
Balance sheet account		to	⇨
Capitalization date		to	⇨
Property classification key		to	⇨
Reason for manual valuation		to	⇨
Acquisition value		to	⇨
Property value		to	⇨
Book value		to	⇨

Figure 6.13 Property Tax Specific Selection Criteria

> **Example**
> Figure 6.14 shows the **Net Worth Tax** tab of an asset master record. This example identifies a building in Seattle with property tax-related information entered in the asset record. Specifically, I have classified the asset as Real Property (what the IRS calls Section 1250 property) using the **Property indicator** field and added a property tax abatement code as the **Manual Val. Reason** (Manual Valuation Reason). Also, I selected the checkbox labeled **Manl net worth tax val.** (Manual net worth tax valuation) to indicate that property taxes for this asset should not be paid on the actual net tax value of the asset, but instead on the amount entered in the field **Man. Net W. Val.** (Manual Net Worth Value). In other words, this field acts as a manual override for the asset's actual values.

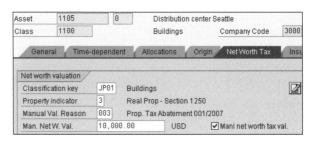

Figure 6.14 Net Worth Tax Information on Asset Master Record

Net Worth Valuation

Asset	SN	Cap.date	Asset description	Σ	Acquis.val.	Rsn	Reason for manual valuation	Σ	Net worth val.	Σ	Book value
1100 ⬚	0	01/01/1993	Production Building 1, New York Plant		2,657,403.00				1,860,168.00		1,863,317.00
Asset Class 1100				▪	2,657,403.00			▪	1,860,168.00	▪	1,863,317.00
Classification key 0				▪▪	2,657,403.00			▪▪	1,860,168.00	▪▪	1,863,317.00
1105	0	11/01/1993	Distribution center Seattle		850,369.00	003	Prop. Tax Abatement 001/2007		10,000.00		596,257.00
Asset Class 1100				▪	850,369.00			▪	10,000.00	▪	596,257.00
Classification key JP01				▪▪	850,369.00			▪▪	10,000.00	▪▪	596,257.00
Company Code 3000				▪▪▪	3,507,772.00			▪▪▪	1,870,168.00	▪▪▪	2,459,574.00

Figure 6.15 Net Worth Valuation Report Layout

Report Output

Figure 6.15 shows the Net Worth Valuation report layout. It includes three value columns: the acquisition cost, the book value, and the manual net worth value.

Notice the values shown for asset number **1105-0**. Because the property tax value was manually entered in the asset master record, the report now shows this amount ($**10,000**) under the **Net worth val.** column instead of the asset's true net book value. Furthermore, the report shows the **Reason for manual valuation** in a separate column.

> **Tip**
>
> Because property taxes are paid to local tax authorities, you should create a sort version that takes into account the physical location of the assets. Companies track the physical location of assets in many different ways, but the most common solutions would derive the assets location from the plant, cost center, or tax jurisdiction code found on the asset master record.

Your tax department can use this report as the basis for their property tax filing, provided that the **Net Worth Tax** tab on the asset master record is maintained accurately.

6.6 Chapter Summary

This chapter discussed the tax-specific reports included in the standard Asset Accounting reporting system. The reports to remember from this chapter are:

▶ **Mid-Quarter Alert Report**
This report analyzes asset acquisitions by fiscal quarter to determine whether more than 40% of all acquisitions fall into the fourth quarter. This would trigger the need for depreciation start date changes and depreciation amount recalculations.

▶ **Total Depreciation Report for IRS Form 4562**
This comprehensive report can be used as the basis for the main IRS tax form 4562. When used together with a proper sort version (i.e., one that sorts and subtotals the assets by useful life), users can simply copy values from the report into the corresponding fields of the IRS form.

▶ **Depreciation Comparison Report**
This report can compare up to three depreciation areas and calculate the depreciation differences between them. The tax department can use this report to compare Federal Tax depreciation amounts with financial book depreciation or Federal Tax amounts with Alternative Minimum depreciation.

▶ **Analysis of Retirement Revenue Report**
This report analyzes retirement postings to determine ordinary versus capital gains or losses for personal and real property assets.

▶ **Net Worth Valuation (Property Tax) Report**
This report is the basis for all property tax reporting in SAP. It includes a manual override functionality to enable accurate property tax reporting

In Chapter 7, you'll learn about two additional reporting tools that let you run asset reports in any currency and to run *what-if* scenarios of asset changes.

7 Reporting Tools

In this chapter, we'll discuss two additional reporting tools that are available on many standard asset reports, but always seem to be overlooked by users. The first tool is *Simulation Versions*, which allows you to simulate the effects of certain changes to asset values. The second tool is *Currency Translation Methods*, which allows you to run asset reports in currencies different from the one assigned to a particular depreciation area. Both reporting tools are simple to set up in configuration and easy to use on the standard report selection screen.

In addition, we'll explore another feature of the Asset Accounting module called *Recalculate Values*. This is not a report, but rather a very important function to ensure that you can produce reliable and up-to-date reports.

7.1 Simulation Versions

Simulation Versions enable you to project asset values in a *what-if* scenario without having to make any changes to the existing asset master records or asset values. Simulation Versions are simple to set up and you can use them with many standard asset reports including the Asset Balances report, the Total Depreciation report, and the Depreciation Simulation report for example.

When to Use Simulation Versions

Let's look at a scenario where you would use a Simulation Version. Let's say that you're considering chang-

ing all assets in the machinery and equipment class from a five-year useful life to a four-year useful life, and you want to know the impact this change will have on annual depreciation expense before committing to it. To find out, you can use a Simulation Version for this scenario without having to make any changes to useful lives and then run a report that will show you the new depreciation expense amounts.

A real-life example

Another good real-life example is the implementation of the 50% bonus depreciation in recent years in the U.S., in which the government allowed a 50% bonus depreciation on certain qualified assets for specific fiscal years. Consequently, many of my consulting clients wanted to know the effect of such changes to their current and future depreciation expense before making any changes to the existing assets. By using a Simulation Version with the Depreciation Forecast report, I was able to quickly analyze the impact of these changes without having to commit to them, and could therefore provide my clients with the answers they needed.

To configure a Simulation Version, use Transaction **OAV7**. Figure 7.1 shows the detail screen for a sample Simulation Version.

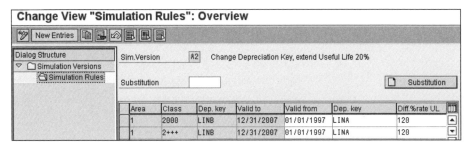

Figure 7.1 Simulation Version Configuration

Asset	SN.	Cap.date	Asset description	DepKy	Life	Ord.dep.Start	Σ Cum.acq.value	Σ Accum.dep.	Σ Start book.v	Σ PlndDep
2180 ▣	0	11/30/1997	Air circulation sys.	LINB	010/000	11/15/1997	37,188.00	33,936.00-	3,252.00	3,252.00-
2181	0	11/30/1997	Granulation unit	LINB	010/000	11/15/1997	47,653.73	43,490.73-	4,163.00	4,163.00-
2182	0	11/12/1997	Test tool	LINB	010/000	11/01/1997	6,199.00	5,684.00-	515.00	515.00-
Company Code 3000						▪	91,040.73 ▪	83,110.73- ▪	7,930.00 ▪	7,930.00-

Figure 7.2 Total Depreciation Report without Simulation Version

Simulation Version Configuration Details

Let's examine the details of the Simulation Version configuration, starting with the first row, shown in Figure 7.1. The simulation will apply to depreciation area **1** and asset class **2000** only. Furthermore, it will apply only to assets with the depreciation key **LINB**. The **Valid to** and **Valid from** dates refer to the assets' capitalization date. In this example, the Simulation Version will apply only to assets with a capitalization date between **01/01/1997** and **12/31/2007**. If an asset fulfills all these criteria, the simulation will change the depreciation key to **LINA** and it will extend the current useful life of the asset by 120%. In other words, if the useful life were 10 years now, it would extend it to 12 years.

Now, look at the second row in Figure 7.1. It is almost identical to the first row, but uses a masking scheme for the asset class field. For example, let's say you have three asset classes:

▶ 2000 – Office Buildings
▶ 2010 – Warehouses
▶ 2020 – Storage Buildings

If you want to make the Simulation Version valid for these three asset classes, you could enter three rows, one for each asset class. A more elegant solution, however, is to use the wildcard character + (plus sign), as shown in the second row. This row specifies that the simulation will apply to all four-digit asset classes that start with **2**.

Figure 7.2 shows the Total Depreciation report for three assets without a Simulation Version. Notice that the current depreciation key for these assets is **LINB**, the useful life is **10** years, and the planned depreciation is **$7,930.00** for the year.

Now let's use a Simulation Version for these three assets. Figure 7.3 shows the selection screen section (**Further settings**) where you can enter the **Simulation version**.

Figure 7.3 Simulation Version Field on the Report Selection Screen

Figure 7.4 shows the same report for the same assets but with the Simulation Version. Notice that the depreciation key has been changed to **LINA**, the useful life is shown as **12** years, and the planned depreciation changed to **$7,586.00** for the year.

As you can see, it's easy to set up *what-if* scenarios for assets using Simulation Versions. The basic configuration screen lets you create simulation rules based on depreciation area, asset class, depreciation key, and capitalization date. If you need additional criteria for more complex simulations, you can use a *Substitution* (also known as a *user exit*) to add your own logic to this functionality via ABAP code.

Asset	SNo.	Cap.date	Asset description	DepKy	Life	Ord.dep.Start	Σ Cum.acq.value	Σ Accum.dep.	Σ Start book.val	Σ PlndDep
2180 ▣	0	11/30/1997	Air circulation sys.	LINA	012/000	11/15/1997	37,188.00	33,936.00-	3,252.00	3,099.00-
2181	0	11/30/1997	Granulation unit	LINA	012/000	11/15/1997	47,653.73	43,490.73-	4,163.00	3,972.00-
2182	0	11/12/1997	Test tool	LINA	012/000	11/01/1997	6,199.00	5,684.00-	515.00	515.00-
Company Code 3000						▪	91,040.73 ▪	83,110.73- ▪	7,930.00 ▪	7,586.00-

Figure 7.4 Total Depreciation Report with Simulation Version

74

7.2 Currency Translation Methods

Currency Translation Methods provide a powerful reporting tool to display asset values in any currency using any exchange rate or logic. You can use these translations methods with many standard SAP reports including the Asset Balances report, the Total Depreciation report, and the Depreciation Simulation report.

Using Currency Translation Methods

To make it easier to follow along, we'll use a previously created asset as an example for this section. The asset, a piece of machinery, has a capitalization date of **01/01/2003** as shown in Figure 7.5.

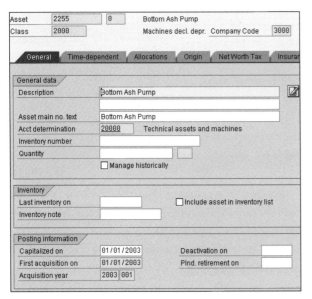

Figure 7.5 An Asset Master Record Showing a Capitalization Date of 1/1/2003

Running a simple Asset Balances report will show the asset's acquisition cost of **$5,500.00**, as shown in Figure 7.6. The report shows the values in U.S. dollars (**USD**) because this is the currency assigned to this particular depreciation area.

Asset Balances - 01 Book deprec.

Report date: 12/31/2007 - Created on: 05/06/2007

Asset	SNo.	Cap.date	Asset description	¤ Acquis.val.	¤ Accum.dep.	¤ Book val.	Crcy
2255	0	01/01/2003	Bottom Ash Pump	5,500.00	2,750.00-	2,750.00	USD
Company Code				5,500.00	2,750.00-	2,750.00	USD

Figure 7.6 Asset Values in U.S. Dollars

Currency Translation Methods Configuration

To configure Currency Translation Methods, you use Transaction **OAW3**. In the example, we will be working with translation method EU, which is the Currency Translation Method you use to convert an asset's U.S. Dollar values into Euro values, as shown in Figure 7.7. Let's look at several of the fields shown in Figure 7.7 in detail:

▶ **Currency**
This is the currency key for the translation. In our example, it is set to Euros (**EUR**).

▶ **Exch. Rate Type**
This is the exchange rate type you want to use with this particular Currency Translation Method. You can set up as many exchange rate types in Financial Accounting as needed.

▶ **Transl. on**
This indicator controls the actual exchange rate logic. It is the most important setting for the currency translation. Available options are explained in Section 1.2.

▶ **Day/Month**
These two fields can only be used when **Free Date** is selected from the **Transl. on** dropdown list. You can then specify the actual calendar date.

Translatn	EU	Euro translation
Currency	EUR	Euro (EMU currency as of 01/01/1999)
Exch. Rate Type	EURO	EMU regulation, fixed exchange rates
Transl. on	1	Capitalization date
Day		
Month		

Figure 7.7 Details for Currency Translation Method EU

Translation On

The **Transl. on** (Translation On) setting tells the system what date (and, correspondingly, what exchange rate) to use for the currency translation. Available options include:

▶ Capitalization date
▶ Free date
▶ Own translation
▶ Acquisition date
▶ Current date

We'll look at each option in detail in this section.

Capitalization Date

As mentioned earlier, our example asset master record shows a capitalization date of 1/1/2003. Now let's check the currency exchange rate table to see what the exchange rate for USD to EUR was on 1/1/2003. As you can see in Figure 7.8, the exchange rate on 1/1/2003 was 1.03610 USD to 1 EUR.

> **Note**
>
> You can use Transaction **OB08** to check the currency exchange rate table in SAP Financial Accounting.

ExRt	ValidFrom	Indir.quot		Ratio(from)	From		Dir.quot.		Ratio (to)	To
EURO	01/01/2007	1.31970	X	1	USD	=		X	1	EUR
EURO	01/01/2006	1.18420	X	1	USD	=		X	1	EUR
EURO	01/01/2005	1.34760	X	1	USD	=		X	1	EUR
EURO	01/01/2004	1.25920	X	1	USD	=		X	1	EUR
EURO	01/01/2003	1.03610	X	1	USD	=		X	1	EUR

Figure 7.8 Currency Exchange Rates

Now let's start a simple Asset Balances report and use the Currency Translation Method **EU** as shown in Figure 7.9.

Settings		
Report date	12/31/2007	
Depreciation area	01	Book deprec.
Sort version	0013	Company code
Translation method	EU	Euro translation

Figure 7.9 Asset Balances Report Selection Screen with Currency Translation Method EU

When you execute the report, you'll see the output shown in Figure 7.10 Notice the report header; it indicates the currency translation to **EUR**. Also, the last column now shows the currency key **EUR**.

Asset Balances - 01 Book deprec.

Report date: 12/31/2007 - Created on: 05/06/2007
Euro translation Currency Key EUR

Asset	SNo.	Cap.date	Asset description	Acquis.val.	Accum.dep.	Book val.	Crcy
2255	0	01/01/2003	Bottom Ash Pump	5,308.37	2,654.18-	2,654.18	EUR
Company code				5,308.37	2,654.18-	2,654.18	EUR

Figure 7.10 Asset Balances Report with Currency Translation to Euro (EUR)

As expected, the currency translation converted the assets' cost of $5,500.00 U.S. Dollars to **5,308.37** Euros, because the exchange rate at the time of the capitalization date 1/1/2003 was 1.03610.

Now, let's try the next option for currency translations, **Free date**.

Free Date

The **Free date** option allows you to enter a specific date of the reporting year. When using the **Free date** option, you have to specify the **Day** and the **Month** of the currency translation, for example, January 1, as shown in Figure 7.11.

Translatn	EU	Euro translation
Currency	EUR	Euro (EMU currency as of 01/01/1999)
Exch. Rate Type	EURO	EMU regulation, fixed exchange rates
Transl. on	2	Free date
Day	1	
Month	1	

Figure 7.11 Free Date Translation as of 1/1

> **Note**
>
> The **Free Date** option only allows you to specify a date and a month, but not a year. Therefore, the currency translation always refers to the reporting fiscal year entered on the selection screen of the report.

When you now execute the report with a reporting date of 12/31/2007, the currency exchange will use the exchange rate that was valid on 1/1 of the reporting year 2007. A quick check of the exchange rate on 1/1/2007 in Figure 7.8 shows the rate as **1.31970**. Consequently, the asset's acquisition cost is now shown as **4,167.61** Euros in Figure 7.12.

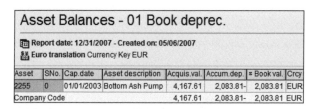

Asset Balances - 01 Book deprec.

Report date: 12/31/2007 - Created on: 05/06/2007
Euro translation Currency Key EUR

Asset	SNo.	Cap.date	Asset description	Acquis.val.	Accum.dep.	Σ Book val.	Crcy
2255	0	01/01/2003	Bottom Ash Pump	4,167.61	2,083.81-	2,083.81	EUR
Company Code				4,167.61	2,083.81-	2,083.81	EUR

Figure 7.12 Asset Values in Euros as of 1/1/2007

Acquisition Date

The **Acquisition date** option refers to the **First Acquisition On** date on the asset master record (unlike the **Capitalization date** option, which, of course refers to the **Capitalization date** on the asset master record).

Under normal circumstances, both dates would always be the same. There are, however, instances where it makes sense to have differences between the two dates, that is, Post Capitalizations (where the **Cap. Date** might be in 2006 but the **First Acq. Date** is in 2007). Other than that, this translation method works just like the **Capitalization date** option explained above.

Current Date

The **Current date** option refers to the physical date on which you are running the report, in other words, today. This option will cause the report to use the most current exchange rate it can find in the currency exchange rate table and, assuming that you update this table on a periodic basis, will produce the most up-to-date reporting values in foreign currencies.

At this point, you might have noticed that we skipped over one translation method, namely, **Own translation**. We're discussing this option last, because it involves your being able to create your own translation method if the other methods we've already looked at don't satisfy your currency translation requirements. So, let's look at this option now.

Own Translation

If none of the above standard options are meeting your translation requirements, you can set the **Transl. on** field to **3 (Own translation)**, as shown in Figure 7.13, to perform your own currency translations. This option works with a user exit where you can provide your own translation logic in the form of custom ABAP code.

To create this user exit, go to Transaction **CMOD** and create a project that uses enhancement project AMGS_001. Make sure that your custom ABAP code is placed into the Include program ZXBADU03.

Translatn	EU	Euro translation
Currency	EUR	Euro (EMU currency as of 01/01/1999)
Exch. Rate Type	EURO	EMU regulation, fixed exchange rates
Transl. on	3	Own translation
Day		
Month		

Figure 7.13 Currency Translation Method with Own Translation (User Exit)

An example for using your own translation would be if you wanted to translate assets as of an important date in the past (i.e., a merger date, a specific asset revaluation date, or any other particular event that had significance for the asset values).

To summarize, Currency Translation Methods allow you to run any asset report in any currency using any translation you want. Now let's take a look at another very important reporting feature — recalculating values.

7.3   Recalculating Values

Whenever you first create and post to an asset master record, the Asset Accounting module automatically calculates the planned depreciation amounts for the fiscal year, based on the depreciation parameters specified in the asset master record and the posting information of the transaction.

For example, say you create an asset master record with a straight-line depreciation key (i.e., the standard SAP depreciation key LINA) and a 10-year useful life. Then, at the beginning of the fiscal year, you post an acquisition transaction of $12,000 to it. Asset Accounting will now automatically calculate a depreciation amount of $1,200 for the year ($12,000 acquisition cost divided by 10 years' useful life).

Then, if you make changes to the asset master record, Asset Accounting also automatically updates the planned depreciation amounts. For example, if you change the useful life of the asset we discussed from 10 years to five years, the system will automatically recalculate the depreciation amount for the fiscal year. In this case, it would increase the planned depreciation amount from $1,200 to $2,400 ($12,000 acquisition cost divided by the new five-year useful life).

In other words, Asset Accounting does a great job of keeping depreciation amounts current. Every time you change the asset master record, the system performs a recalculation of depreciation values (even if you change things that have no impact on depreciation at all, i.e., changing the asset's description).

However, as good as this automatic recalculation works when asset master record changes are made, it doesn't work this way when you make changes in configuration that impact the depreciation calculation logic. Let's look at this in more detail.

Making Changes to the Calculation Logic Configuration
Earlier in our example, we mentioned the standard SAP depreciation key LINA, which is configured to use a straight-line depreciation calculation. If you were to change this calculation logic in the configuration transactions, the system would not perform an automatic recalculation of the asset's depreciation amounts.

In order to update the calculated depreciation amounts for assets in these situations, Asset Accounting provides the function called **Recalculate values**. You can run this program for many assets concurrently, or for just a single asset. To recalculate values for a single asset, use the Asset Change transaction (Transaction **AS02**), enter the asset number, and select **Edit • Recalculate values**, as shown in Figure 7.14.

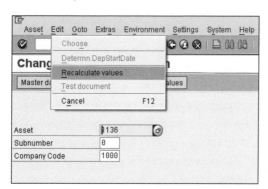

Figure 7.14 Recalculate Values from Transaction AS02

Figure 7.15 shows the message you'll see after the system successfully recalculates the asset's values.

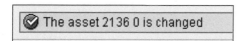

Figure 7.15 Message Shown After an Asset Recalculation

Tip
If you don't want to commit to any asset value recalculation just yet, you can simulate the recalculation for a single asset in the Asset Explorer transaction. To do so, go to Transaction **AW01N**, enter an asset number, and click the icon labeled **Recalculate dep.** (the icon looks like a calculator). This will execute a simulated

recalculation without any actual database updates taking place.

Recalculating Values for Several or All Assets
If you want to recalculate the values for several or all assets, you can use the following Recalculate Values program:

▶ **Menu Path**
Accounting • Financial Accounting • Fixed Assets • Environment • Recalculate Values
▶ **Transaction Code**
AFAR
▶ **Technical Report Name**
RAAFAR00

Figure 7.16 shows the selection screen for this program. You can limit the recalculation program by **Company code**, **Main asset number**, **Depreciation area**, and **FROM fiscal year**. This lets you recalculate the tax depreciation for a specific fiscal year only, for example, without impacting other depreciation areas.

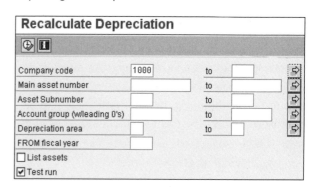

Figure 7.16 Selection Screen for Recalculation Program

You can also **List assets** (an option you can select) to see each individual asset on the report output; otherwise, the report output will be on a summary level. And, as with just about all other functions in Asset Accounting, it would be prudent to run this program in **Test run** mode first before making any actual database updates. A test run allows you to review any potential changes without actually updating the asset database. Once you run the program, the output will look similar to that shown in Figure 7.17.

CoCd	Year	Area	Acct.det	Asset	SNo.	Description	Dep. Type	Σ	Old	Σ	New	Σ	Diff.
1000	2006	01	20000	2161	0	3-ton press	Ord.depreciation		434.33-		435.33-		1.00
				2164	0	Assembly line	Ord.depreciation		4,178.33-		4,179.33-		1.00
			20000					■	4,612.66-	■	4,614.66-	■	2.00
		01						■■	4,612.66-	■■	4,614.66-	■■	2.00
	2007		20000	2161	0	3-ton press	Ord.depreciation		109.00-		108.00-		1.00-
				2164	0	Assembly line	Ord.depreciation		1,045.00-		1,044.00-		1.00-
			20000					■	1,154.00-	■	1,152.00-	■	2.00-
		01						■■	1,154.00-	■■	1,152.00-	■■	2.00-

Figure 7.17 Recalculate Values Output

Notice that the list shows the annual values for each asset (if **List assets** was selected on the selection screen), lists the old and the new depreciation amounts, and even calculates the difference in depreciation.

> **Note**
>
> It is important to understand that the Recalculate Values program neither changes any posted amounts nor creates any postings. It merely ensures that the *planned* depreciation amounts are based on the current configuration settings.

To ensure that your depreciation for any given year is correctly calculated, you should run the Recalculate Values program at least once a year, just prior to the year-end closing procedures for Asset Accounting. I do, however, recommend running this program more often (i.e., monthly, as part of the month-end closing procedures) to my clients.

7.4 Chapter Summary

In this chapter, you learned that Simulation Versions and Currency Translation Methods in Asset Accounting reporting can be set up easily and provide a flexible way to enhance the standard reports. You also learned that

the recalculation of asset values ensures that the planned depreciation amounts properly reflect the current configuration settings. Key points to remember from this chapter include:

▶ Simulation Versions can show the impact of simulated depreciation term changes, including depreciation key and useful life changes, without having to make any changes to the existing asset data.

▶ Currency Translation Methods enable you to display asset reports in any currency using any translation logic. Standard currency translation options include currency translations as of the capitalization date, the acquisition date, today's date, or a specified date. If these options are insufficient for a specific user requirement, you can create a user exit and provide your own currency translation logic.

▶ To ensure that depreciation is correct at all times, it is important to run the Recalculate Values program at least once a year before the year-end closing. Personally, I suggest running this program on a monthly basis.

In Chapter 8, the final chapter, you'll be introduced to the Asset Explorer, which is a powerful tool for analyzing a single asset's values.

8 Asset Explorer

The main Asset Accounting reports are the best way to report asset information and values for a large number of assets. Sometimes, however, you may want to analyze only a single asset. In those circumstances, the *Asset Explorer* is the optimal tool of choice.

8.1 The Asset Explorer Screen

To access the Asset Explorer, use Transaction **AW01N**. Figure 8.1 shows the basic Asset Explorer screen for an asset. We'll now look at the different sections of the fairly busy Asset Explorer screen in more detail, starting with

the top part of the screen shown in Figure 8.2. Here, you can enter the **Company Code**, **Asset** main number and subnumber for the asset you want to analyze, and the specific **Fiscal year** for which you want to display the values.

Depreciation Areas

Next, let's look at the upper left section of the Asset Explorer screen. It displays all available **Depreciation Areas** for this asset, as shown in detail in Figure 8.3. Simply click a depreciation area to switch the asset value display from one depreciation area to another.

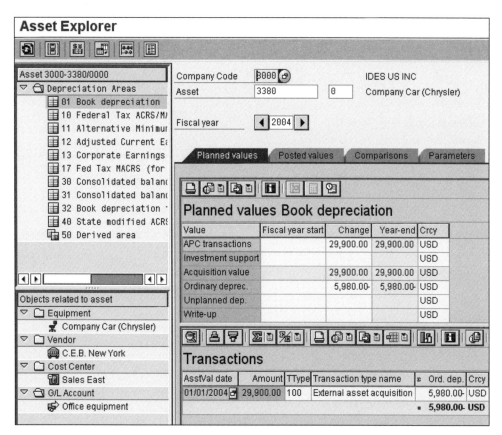

Figure 8.1 Asset Explorer Basic Screen

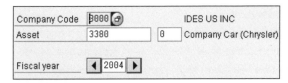

Figure 8.2 Asset Number and Fiscal Year

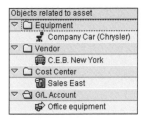

Figure 8.3 Depreciation Areas

> **Tip**
>
> The section that shows the company code and asset number at the top of this screen is actually a button. Click it and you will be sent to Transaction **AS03** (Display Asset Master record).

Related Objects

Directly below the **Depreciation Areas** section is a box for related objects. Figure 8.4 shows that this asset is assigned to an **Equipment** master record **Company Car (Chrysler)** (in the Plant Maintenance (PM) module); that the asset was bought from **Vendor C.E.B. New York**; that it belongs to **Cost Center Sales East**; and that it posts its values to **G/L Account Office equipment**. You can double-click each of these related objects to access the corresponding master data display transactions.

Figure 8.4 Objects Related to Asset

Asset Transactions

Directly to the right of the related objects section is the **Transactions** area shown in detail in Figure 8.5. This area shows all posted asset transactions for the fiscal year. You

can double-click any asset transaction to display more detail about the posting and, if available, even display the document in the financial accounting system.

Transactions

AsstVal date	Amount	TType	Transaction type name	Ord. dep.	Crcy
01/01/2004	29,900.00	100	External asset acquisition	5,980.00-	USD
				5,980.00-	**USD**

Figure 8.5 Asset Transactions for the Fiscal Year

Asset Values

Directly to the right of the **Depreciation Area** section is the section that contains main asset value information, as shown in detail in Figure 8.6.

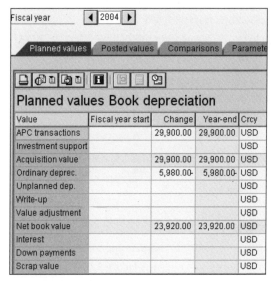

Figure 8.6 Asset Value Display

This section shows all available asset values in three columns:

- ▶ **Fiscal year start**
  This column shows the values as of the beginning of the fiscal year displayed.
- ▶ **Change**
  This column shows the summary of all transactions of the fiscal year.
- ▶ **Year-end**
  This column shows the resulting values as of the end of the fiscal year.

As you can see in Figure 8.6, this particular asset had no values at the beginning of the fiscal year and therefore, was acquired during the fiscal year displayed. Also notice the various tabs on this screen, shown in Figure 8.7, which we'll look at in more detail.

Figure 8.7 Asset Value Tabs

▶ **Planned values**
This tab shows the planned depreciation values for the asset (as opposed to the posted values)

▶ **Posted values**
This tab shows the actual posted depreciation amounts for the asset. For example, Figure 8.8 shows the monthly depreciation postings for the asset.

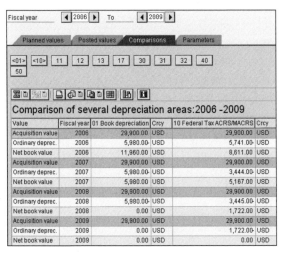

Figure 8.8 Posted Depreciation

▶ **Comparisons**
This tab allows you to compare multiple depreciation areas for several fiscal years. Figure 8.9 shows the comparison for depreciation area 01 and 10 for fiscal years 2006 through 2009.

Figure 8.9 Depreciation Comparisons Tab

▶ **Parameters**
This tab shows the depreciation calculation parameters for this asset; specifically, it includes the depreciation key (**Dep. Key**), useful life (**Useful life**), and depreciation start date (**Ord.dep.start date**), as shown in Figure 8.10.

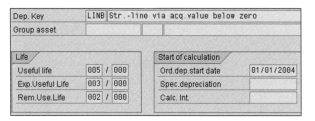

Figure 8.10 Depreciation Parameters

8.2 Asset Explorer Simulations

Another great feature of the Asset Explorer is that you can use it to simulate the following:

▶ Changes to depreciation parameters
▶ Asset transactions

Simulating Changes to Depreciation Parameters
Simulating depreciation parameter changes (akin to the Simulation Versions) is easy in the Asset Explorer. Click the **Switch on Simulation** icon (F9) shown in Figure 8.11 to turn on the simulation mode.

Figure 8.11 Switch on Simulation Mode Icon

You know that you are in simulation mode when the description of the transaction changes to **Asset Explorer Simulation**, as shown in Figure 8.12.

Asset Explorer Simulation

Figure 8.12 Simulation Mode

Now you can easily change the depreciation parameters on the **Parameters** tab. Figure 8.13 shows the parameter fields available for input.

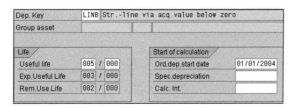

Figure 8.13 Change Parameters in Simulation Mode

Simulating Asset Transactions

In addition to changing the depreciation parameters in simulation mode, you can also simulate asset transactions. When you are on the **Planned values** tab, click the **Trans. Simulation** icon in the lower right portion of the screen (it looks like an abacus) to enter a simulated transaction for the asset. For example, Figure 8.14 shows a simulated asset retirement transaction.

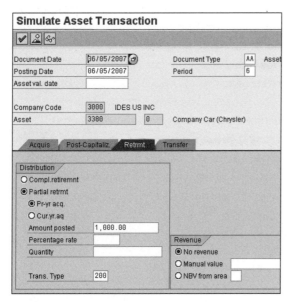

Figure 8.14 Simulated Asset Retirement

> **Note**
> Simulating asset transactions is a powerful feature that is only available in the Asset Explorer.

8.3 Currency Translations

Just as you can use Currency Translation Methods in asset reports, you can also use them in the Asset Explorer. To get started, click the icon **Translate currency amounts** shown in Figure 8.15 and then select the Currency Trans-

lation Method of your choice. This will display all values in the Asset Explorer in a different currency using the exchange rate you want.

Figure 8.15 Calling the Currency Translation Method in Asset Explorer

8.4 Depreciation Calculation

One of the most important features of the Asset Explorer is that it allows you to display the logic for depreciation calculations. In other words, whenever you find yourself asking why or how the system calculated a particular depreciation amount, you can use this function to analyze the parameters the system used in its calculation routines. To use this feature, select the **Planned values** tab and click the **Display dep. calculation** icon shown in Figure 8.16.

Figure 8.16 Display dep. Calculation Icon

The next screen that displays, shown in Figure 8.17, includes the details for all depreciation calculation parameters from rounding rules to the order of depreciation calculation, and many other important calculation routines.

The information in this screen will tell you exactly how the system arrived at the depreciation amount shown. Specifically, this screen shows you the **Base Value** for the depreciation calculation (**$29,900.00**), the **Percentage** rate (**0.200000**), and the resulting calculated depreciation amount (**$5,980.00**). You could even drill down deeper by using the following buttons:

▶ **Calculation Parameters**
This button displays the individual parameters that have been configured for the depreciation key that's used on the asset master record.

▶ **Depreciation Terms**
This button displays the depreciation terms from the asset master record, such as the depreciation key used, depreciation start date, etc.

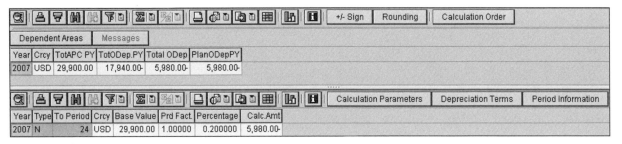

Figure 8.17 Depreciation Calculation Parameters

▶ **Period Information**

This button displays the number of periods for the depreciation calculation, including the useful life and expired useful life for the asset.

> **Tip**
>
> The Display Depreciation Calculation function only works for open fiscal years!

8.5 Chapter Summary

The Asset Explorer is a powerful tool you can use to display and analyze a single asset's values. It offers a variety of functions that combine the best of many individual asset reports. For example, the Asset Explorer shows planned and posted values, supports currency translations and simulation versions, and even enables you to simulate asset transactions (such as retirements, transfers, etc.). Furthermore, the Asset Explorer can forecast depreciation for future fiscal years.

One of the most important features of the Asset Explorer, however, is its ability to display the deprecia-

tion calculation logic, which helps you to understand why and how the system has calculated a certain depreciation amount.

8.6 Guide Summary

This completes our discussion of Asset Accounting reporting. Hopefully, after reading this guide, you have learned a lot about the basic Asset Accounting reporting system. You now know how to use the different report functions to produce accurate and meaningful asset reports, as well as how to use the assorted reporting tools to enhance the standard asset reports.

With this knowledge, you should be able to fulfill almost all reporting requirements for fixed assets without having to create custom reports or queries. If you ever find yourself in a position where no standard asset report meets your requirements, you should consider a Business Warehouse report or custom SQVI query as your next best alternative.

A   Glossary

ABAP Query   An ABAP reporting tool that enables a user to create his own report without having to know any programming. The ABAP Query tool uses a graphical interface and builds the ABAP code needed for the report automatically in the background.

Acquisition and Production Cost (APC)   Commonly referred to as the *asset's cost*.

Advanced Business Application Programming (ABAP)   This is the SAP programming language.

Asset Accounting   Subsidiary ledger to the General Ledger (G/L) used to manage fixed assets. Also known as *Fixed Assets* and the *Asset Management* module.

Asset Balance Reports   These types of reports show the asset's values as of a specific date (the reporting date). *See also* Asset Transaction Reports.

Asset Class   A criteria to classify assets by type according to legal or business requirements. Typical asset classes include Machinery and Equipment, Fixtures and Furniture, etc.

Asset Explorer   A tool used to perform comprehensive analysis, reporting, and simulation for fixed assets. The Asset Explorer connects the asset master record, asset values, asset transactions, and additional related objects (such as cost centers, plants, G/L accounts) in one single transaction.

Asset History Sheet   A report that shows the progress of an asset's transactional history from the beginning of the fiscal year through the reporting date. This report can be configured in accordance with the users' specific requirements.

Asset Number   A number that consists of the main number and the subnumber. Together with the company code, these two numbers uniquely identify an asset master record in the SAP system.

Asset Transaction Reports   These types of reports show the transactions posted to an asset during the reporting period (usually beginning of the year to reporting date). *See also* Asset Balance Reports.

Asset Under Construction (AuC)   An asset that is in the process of being completed and is not in service yet. Typically, AuCs are shown on a separate account in the balance sheet and therefore are assigned to a special asset class.

Asset Value Date   The date of an asset transaction from the Asset Accounting point of view. This date can be different than the posting date and document date and can even be in accounting periods that have already been closed. However, all dates must be within the same fiscal year.

Barcode   A physical item used to tag, identify, and track fixed assets. Usually applied as a sticker or label directly to the physical piece of equipment. *See also* Radio Frequency Identification Tag (RFID).

Book Value   The asset's net value as of a specific date. Also referred to as *Net Book Value* or *Net Tax Value*, depending on the depreciation area used to calculate the amount.

BW   Business Warehouse. A separate SAP application used to extract information from the SAP system for further analysis and reporting.

Capitalization Date   Each asset master record can have only a single capitalization date. It represents the date on which the asset was placed into service.

Change Document   A document in SAP that records changes made to master records or transactions. The document includes information on the change itself (before and after values), date/timestamps, and user information.

Cost Center   An organizational unit within the controlling area that represents a location where costs are incurred and tracked (e.g., asset depreciation is typically posted to cost centers).

Currency Translation Methods   A reporting tool used in Asset Accounting for translating asset values to another currency using various exchange rates. Currency Translation Methods can be used on the selection screen of Asset Accounting reports.

Depreciation Area   An area that tracks the values for an asset for a specific purpose (e.g., for tax, financial balance sheet, or consolidation purposes). An asset can have up to 99 depreciation areas, each with its own set of asset values.

Depreciation, Depletion, and Amortization (DDA)   Commonly referred to as the *asset's depreciation*.

Depreciation Key   A key to calculate depreciation amounts for an asset's depreciation area. The depreciation key controls the calculation of depreciation, interest, and scrap values, and can be assigned to the depreciation within an asset record.

Depreciation Start Date   Each depreciation area for an asset has its own depreciation start date. The start date is when the depreciation calculation for this asset and depreciation started. The date is usually derived from the capitalization date (but the dates don't have to be the same due to different depreciation calculation requirements in the different depreciation areas).

Dynamic Selections   User-defined selections to access the Logical Database. Dynamic selections allow users to further define selection criteria for efficient data retrieval.

Investment Measure   An Internal Order, Work Breakdown Structure (WBS) element, or Appropriation Request used in a capital project with the goal of producing or capitalizing a fixed asset.

Logical Database   A collection of SAP programs designed to retrieve data efficiently for various application areas. The Logical Database ADA is used extensively with all Asset Accounting reports.

Radio Frequency Identification Tag (RFID)   A small computer chip used to tag, identify, and track fixed assets. *See also* Barcode

Reporting Date   Most Asset Accounting reports require a reporting date that is the date from which asset values are being calculated.

SAPscript   A tool used to manage, design, and edit text forms that can then be printed from various SAP transactions.

Selection Screen   Every Asset Accounting report starts with a Selection screen that enables users to enter specific parameters for the report and other limitations in order to produce a meaningful report. Selection screens usually come in a short, abbreviated version with limited selection criteria, as well as a full version that includes all selection fields.

Simulation Version   A reporting tool in Asset Accounting used to analyze depreciation parameter changes and their impact on depreciation calculation without having to make actual changes to the asset master records.

Sort Versions A tool used to sort and subtotal asset reports. Can be configured easily and is a critical component for producing meaningful asset reports.

Transaction Type A key used in Asset Accounting for every asset posting. It classifies each transaction into various categories (i.e., acquisition, retirement, and transfer), and can then be used in reporting to produce corresponding transaction reports (e.g., an acquisition report, retirement report, etc.).

Useful Life The expected time period over which an asset is to be used and depreciated. The useful life varies by asset type and depreciation area.

Work Breakdown Structure (WBS) Element A hierarchical outline of a project and description of individual tasks within a project definition.

B Resources

Additional information available on the Internet related to SAP Asset Accounting:

▶ **Michael Management Corporation**
www.michaelmanagement.com
This is the author's company's website. Michael Management Corporation is an SAP consulting, development, and training firm that specializes in Asset Accounting, Project System, and Investment Management issues. This website offers articles, presentations, and online training courses for SAP Asset Accounting.

▶ **SAP Online Documentation**
http://help.sap.com
The online help documentation for the entire SAP system is available at this website.

▶ **SAP Developer Network**
www.sdn.sap.com
SAP's Developer Network (SDN) is a large online community for SAP developers, users, analysts, and consultants. Membership is free.

▶ **Internal Revenue Service (IRS)**
www.irs.gov/formspubs/index.html?portlet=3
All tax forms listed in this guide were downloaded from this link.

▶ **Financial Accounting Standards Board (FASB)**
www.fasb.org/
This website offers hundreds of rules, regulations, and articles around accounting standards.

▶ **America's SAP Users' Group (ASUG)**
www.asug.com/
The world's largest SAP user group's website offers a wealth of information and networking opportunities. Membership is required.

▶ **Wellesley Information Services**
www.wispubs.com/sap/
Wellesley Information Services (WIS) is an independent provider of information to professionals who deploy, manage, support, configure, and customize SAP solutions. This website offers a large variety of SAP-related newsletters and expert magazines.

Index

ISBN   978-1-59229-143-4

1st edition 2007

© 2007 by Galileo Press GmbH

SAP PRESS is an imprint of Galileo Press,

Boston (MA), USA

Bonn, Germany

Acquisitions Editor Jawahara Saidullah
Developmental Editor Jutta VanStean
Copy Editor Nancy Etscovitz, UCG, Inc., Boston, MA
Cover Design Vera Brauner
Production Iris Warkus
Printed in Germany